pe 41

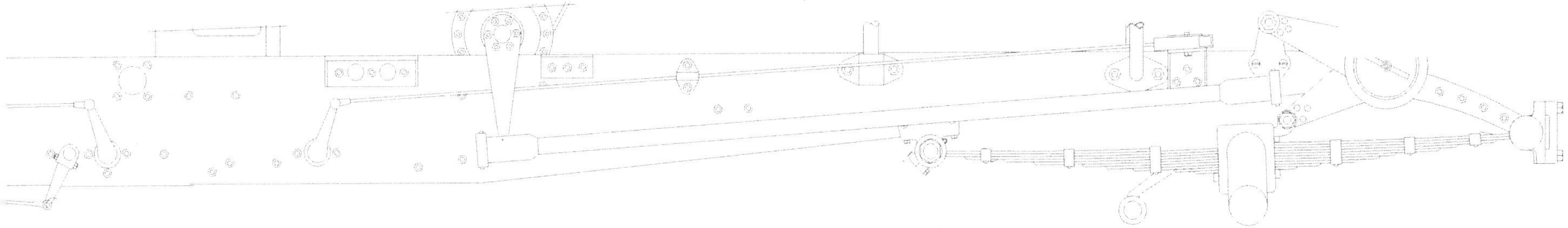

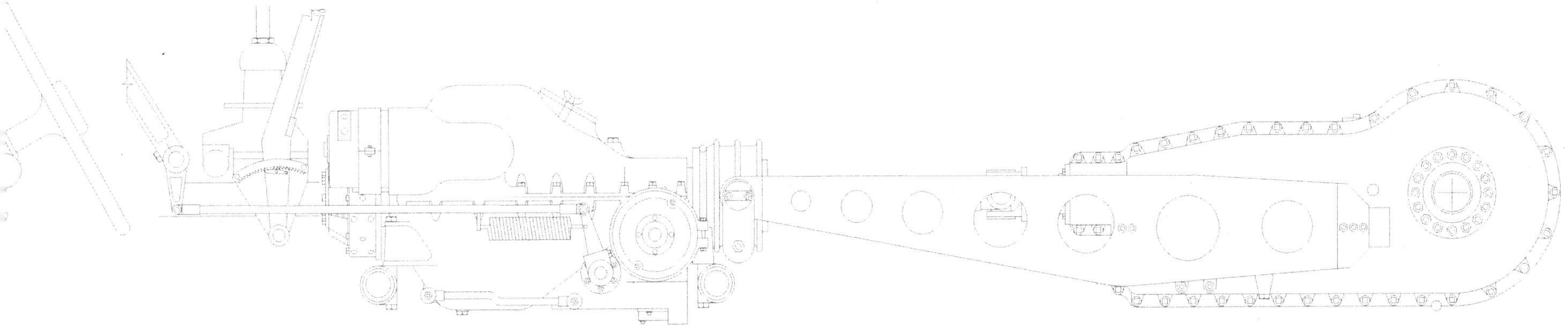

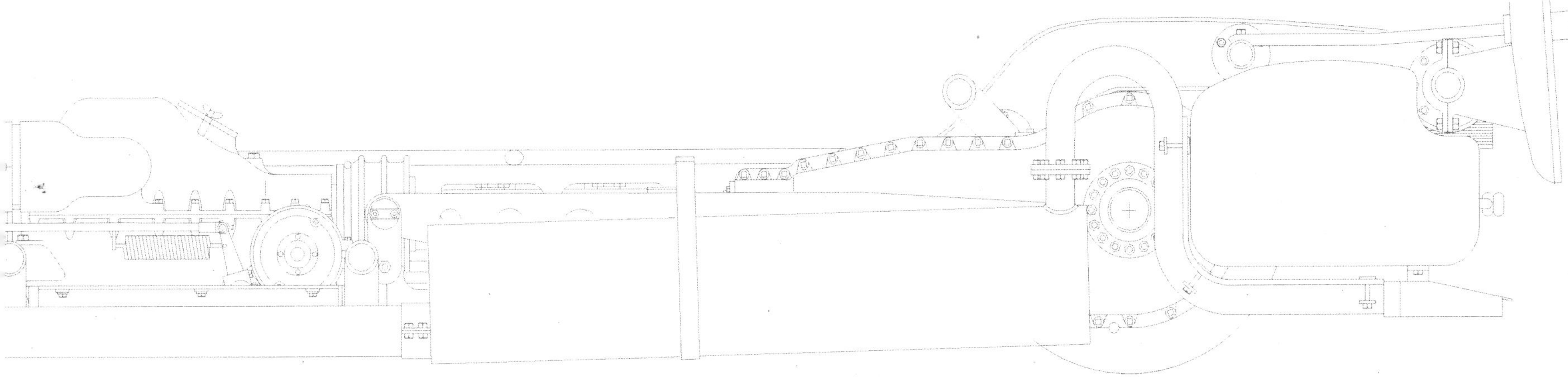

Art of the Automobile
in miniature

Phyllis and Gerald A. Wingrove MBE, model engineers with one-fifteenth scale Duesenberg chassis.

Art of the Automobile in miniature

The Works of Gerald and Phyllis Wingrove – Model Engineers

Gerald A. Wingrove MBE

Foreword by James Knight

The Crowood Press

First published in 2003 by
The Crowood Press Ltd
Ramsbury, Marlborough
Wiltshire SN8 2HR

www.crowood.com

British Library Cataloguing-in-Publication Data
A catalogue record for this book is available from the British Library.

ISBN 1 86126 632 4

Typefaces used: Bembo (main text) and Parisian (captions and headings).

Typeset and designed by D & N Publishing
Lowesden Business Park, Hungerford, Berkshire.

Printed and bound in Singapore by Craft Print International.

Contents

Acknowledgements

To Phyllis
For her enthusiasm and unfailing support for all that I undertake.

I wish to express my sincere thanks to the very many people, collectors, engineers, researchers and restorers, whose most generous help and enthusiasm have made it possible for both Phyllis and me to be able to create the work illustrated in the following pages. In particular, I must thank Randy Mason and the staff and administration of the Henry Ford Museum & Greenfield Village in Dearborn, Michigan, USA, for allowing us free access to the cars and the Museum archives, to Briggs Cunningham and Bill Harrah for making their respective Bugatti Royales freely available for our research, and David Pfeiffer at the National Archives for his invaluable help. Also, and in equal proportion, our grateful thanks go to Don Williams, Jim Crank, Hugh Conway, John Frizzell, Norey Korhil Fuchs, Phil Reilley, Carol Edkins, Bill Bizer, O.A. Bunny Phillips, Fred Roe, David Brimson, Alf Helling, Andy Rheault, Griffith Borgeson, Horst Lattke, Jonathan Harley, Alain Glew, Randy Ema, Richie Clyne, Don Howell, Alain de Cadenet, Dave Holls, Eric Eckermann, Dick Crosthwaite, John Gardner, Bob Fabris, Josh B. Malks, Simon Moore, Tony Merrick, Paul Grist, Scott Bergan, Jeff Orwig, John Bentley, Dr Hannelore Theodor, Tony Brown, Henry Austin Clark, Roger Barlow, David V. Uihlein and R. Willis Leith Jr.

For the use of photographs as follows:
Clive Friend FBIPP: photos on pages 2, 23, 25, 27, 29, 31, 33, 35, 37, 41, 43, 47, 49, 51, 53, 57, 59, 73, 75, 77, 79, 81, 83, 85, 87, 89, 91 (top), 95, 100, 101, 119, 121, 123; Ludwig Weinberger Jr: photo on page 60 (top left); Eric Eckermann: photo on page 60 (right); Rob Ingles: photos on pages 91 (bottom), 107, 109 (top); W. Willis Leith Jr: photo on page 65; Horst Lattke: photo on page 62 (bottom), 68 (bottom right); from the National Automotive History Collection, Detroit Public Library, Charles Chayne Collection: photos on pages 64, 66, 67 (top right), 68 (top left); from the collection of the Henry Ford Museum & Greenfield Village: photos on pages 60 (bottom left), 61 (bottom), 62 (top left and right), 66.

Gerald A. Wingrove MBE

Foreword

WHEN ASKED TO WRITE THIS FOREWORD TO GERALD'S LATEST BOOK I immediately glazed over, since so much has already been written about this master craftsman whose extraordinary work I personally regard with complete awe.

So, since my own involvement is from a more commercial angle I thought I should focus on this aspect as it would be new and fresh.

I have handled Wingrove models for the past twenty years. They very rarely come to market although as many as have been built still survive. The simple answer is that once acquired they are greatly admired and collectors hardly ever part with them. This is truly a defining testament to both the man and the model maker.

When I first met Gerald some ten years ago I met an uncompromising man whose standards and attention to detail were obviously second to none. There is, however, an unsung hero – his wife Phyllis – who lays the groundwork for such detail. For it is Phyllis who will research, catalogue and survey a life-size vehicle from a multitude of angles in order to produce exquisite scale drawings. And it is from these drawings that Gerald's craftsmanship then creates such an exacting model.

To be in a position to offer a Wingrove model for sale really is something special. As I have said before the opportunity physically to handle one of Gerald's models is such a rare occurrence that to target and receive enquiries about it from knowledgeable and learned clients is more than just an auctioneering pleasure, it is a privilege.

Art of the Automobile in Miniature provides a wonderful insight into the remarkable partnership of Phyllis and Gerald Wingrove and is by itself a highly collectible addition to any motoring library.

James Knight
Director
Motoring Department
Bonhams Auctioneers

River view of Buckler's Hard shipyard (model), 3 June 1803, Hampshire, England.

Toy development: prototype for Dinky toys (No.717) Boeing 737.

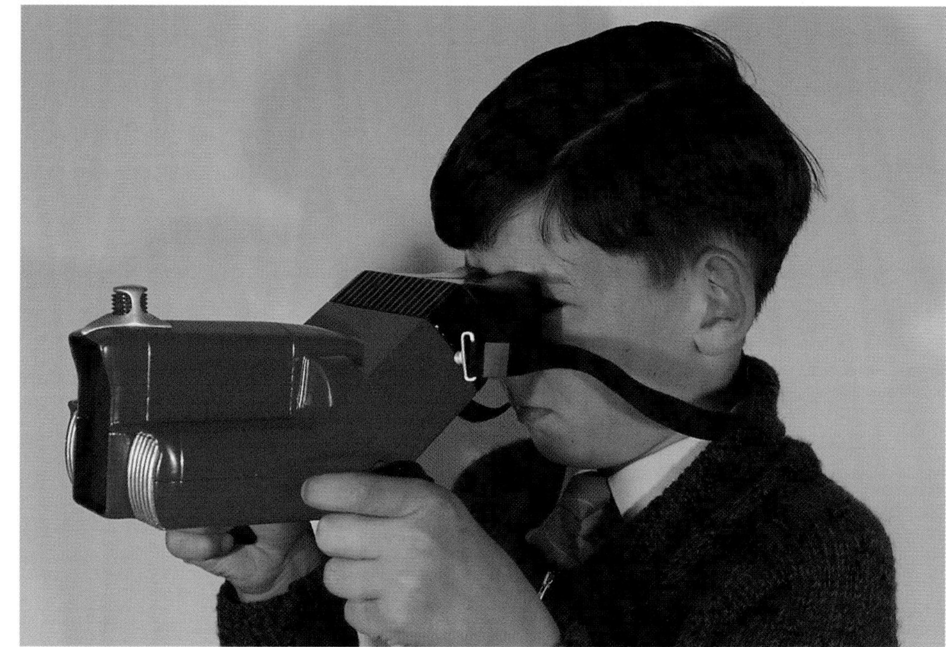

Film props – son Mark with the full-size Mysteron detector, made for the film, *Captain Scarlet and the Mysterons.*

The Early Years

AFTER A LIFETIME IN MODEL ENGINEERING, INCLUDING OVER THREE decades specializing in building automobile miniatures for some of the most discerning collectors in the world, I feel I may now have an understanding of what 'The Art of the Automobile' is, or at least to be aware of it, and to be able to embody it in miniature form. However, before presenting my canvas, I should perhaps establish my credentials.

My fondest memories of early childhood invariably involve making things, either with my father, a French polisher by trade who had a woodshed (old English for a 'den') well stocked with hand tools, in which I spent most of my spare time. Whereas some people may have been born with silver spoons in their mouths, I must have come into this world with a penknife in my hand. If I was not engaged in whittling a piece of wood into some shape or other, then much of my time was spent in taking my toys apart to see how they were made.

It would seem that having always had a fascination for the smaller things in life, the larger ones have been allowed to take their own course. Living as we did with a small river running past the front of the family home, and having a fish pond in the garden, it was probably inevitable that model boats and ships would become a part of my life. So it was that in my early teens, an interest grew in the sailing ships of the eighteenth and nineteenth centuries. My fascination was in the intricacies of the design and, when building a miniature, how so many nondescript parts could make into a whole which then took on a character of its own.

Having built about a dozen sailing ship models, the last and final examples were incorporated into the Buckler's Hard 25 sq ft diorama. This illustrated two ships of the line, the *Swiftsure* and the *Euryalus*, under construction, and a typical day in the life of a village shipyard at the time of Nelson, namely the third of June 1803, with man and beast going about their daily tasks. The model was built for Lord Montagu of Beaulieu as the centrepiece for his new museum at the village of Buckler's Hard in Hampshire, England, and is on public display there. Lessons learnt in building this were that it was possible to put life into the most lifeless of materials, even on the tiny scale of one to two hundredths, which was the scale of this very large model. Most of the other ship models were sold at auction and are now in collections in Europe and the USA.

After a very rudimentary wartime education, in which I appeared to shine at very little and learn even less, except that 'a lever is a rigid bar that moves about a fixed point called the fulcrum' (knowledge for which I am still trying to find a use), school ceased at fourteen and several jobs followed in quick succession. The first was in film processing 'D & P' (developing and printing), as it was called before the digital age, in the backroom of a local photographers. This proved to be very useful in later years, as most of the more than 10,000 detail photos taken to assist in the drafting of scale plans for the work shown here were processed in a home-built photographic darkroom, which made for great savings in overall costs in the early years of getting started as a model engineer. This was followed by a short spell in glass blowing, a diversion I have, as yet, not been able to develop, followed by fourteen years as a lathe turner in light engineering. The latter entailed making small parts in brass, steel and aluminium on a lathe in a production-line environment. It proved invaluable in later years, primarily in learning how to produce precision parts in metal with the utmost accuracy in minimal time with the smallest number of tools. The relevance of this is that it took place at a time in light engineering before the introduction of 'work study'.

In the early years, one was taught how to operate a lathe, set speeds and feeds for various operations and metals, and to grind one's own tools to produce a part most efficiently. If you showed interest, you could become very skilled, and I became very, very interested. The fascination was in being able to produce the most complex of parts with extreme precision, from a block of hard metal, and repeat the process with ease. Consider a car engine and imagine learning the secrets of being able to make this from basic blocks of metal with your own two hands and a couple of machine tools, and you may perceive my fascination.

When 'work study' was introduced in the late 1950s, it was on the basis of having unskilled labour operating the lathes, milling, drilling and grinding machines in an engineering machine shop. It entailed the management bringing in a team of 'so-called' engineers who had undertaken a course in theory from 'the book' that would determine the speeds and feeds and general setting of the machines for specific jobs, from nuts and bolts to a complicated engine component. The machinist was now provided with detailed instructions regarding every aspect of how to set up his machine, with all his tools ready ground for him (i.e. sharpened and shaped) according to 'the book', so that the most unskilled person off the street could be shown how to turn the right handles on the machine and so produce the required part without breaking too many tools or cutting off a finger. When the said machine was set up as per the work-study directive, the machinist was timed with a stopwatch to see if he could produce the part in the estimated time according to 'the book'. If he could not, he was shown how to make a reasonable attempt and then asked to accept the time. If the estimated time was given as ten minutes, then the machinist would be expected to be able to make the part in five or six minutes. The difference between these two times, that is, four minutes, was paid for as a bonus, and was called 'piecework', and this bonus could form up to 50 per cent of the machinist's weekly wage.

There was much objection to the new work-study system from the shop floor when it was introduced, to the extent that when the work-study man came into the machine shop with his clipboard and stopwatch, all the machinists would down tools and march out on strike until he left. Most of these unfortunate officials appeared to have come into engineering from another world, and knew nothing about general engineering other than what they had learned from 'the book' before being let loose on the machine shop floor. The young man assigned to my own work had had a past life as a carpet layer – so one can imagine the resentment that was felt on the shop floor when highly skilled men with decades of experience were told how to do their job by such people, especially when, in most cases, they could produce a better job by the old tried and tested ways in a shorter time.

In reality, the management was facing a lack of skilled machinists, so had no choice but to introduce the scheme. Once the work-study man had completed his official visit, the ever-diminishing number of highly skilled machinists would be allowed to retool their jobs. It meant, for the lucky few, that the operation that had taken six minutes when it had been allowed ten, might now be reduced to just two minutes, after a judicious amount of remaking of tools and resetting of the machine. The end result would be a bonus time of eight minutes per part, thus improving one's wage by 30 per cent. It presented a good incentive to educate oneself well in the intricacies of working machine tools to their utmost efficiency, and is, I believe, one of the keys to my success as a freelance model engineer.

Two years of National Service in the RAF provided an interlude of sorts during this period, which also helped to shape my future, as most of it was spent in the Canal Zone in Egypt just after the Suez crisis. Work involved the repair of aircraft airframe metalwork, mainly in aluminium. However, because of our location in the desert and the high temperatures in the day, we were only expected to work from about four in the morning until midday, with the rest of the day free. The political situation was still tense and it was not safe to go out of camp unless in a party of ten or more with an armed guard, and then only down to the Great Bitter Lakes on the Suez Canal to go swimming. Preferring to be on the water than in it or under it, most of my ample spare time during those eighteen months was spent in building model aircraft, as the full-sized ones were very abundant.

It was my good fortune to be stationed at RAF Fayed in the centre of the Canal Zone, which was also the emergency airport for Cairo. The interest in building model aircraft was not to fly them, but to scratch-build static, highly detailed models of civilian aircraft such as the de Havilland Comet and Bristol Britannia – airliners that we had the good fortune to see at close hand from time to time. After returning to my old employer, and after the introduction of work study, the management started to reign in the loose cannons who were making hay with the new system. During this time, I had been provided with a splendid new machine, all bells and whistles, that had served me very well for a number of years, and which I could almost make sing. Then one day there was a cloud of acrid smoke from its rear, and all was silent – the large electric motor had finally succumbed. By this time, the large engineering machine shops were being revolutionized yet again with the introduction of computer-controlled, all-purpose machine tools. Seeing no future in being at the beck and call of a computer gave me the impetus to take the plunge at thirty-two years of age to offer myself as a freelance model engineer to whoever could make use of my time and skills.

After the abundant free time in Egypt building models with minimal tools and the odd bits and pieces of materials I could scrounge from the scrap box and stores, I felt it was worth learning more about model making in general, and maybe considering it as a most enjoyable full-time occupation. On returning to civilian life, I spent all of my spare time reading books and asking questions from any quarter that could provide useful information on the many and varied techniques of working all manner of materials and finishes. When fate determined the time to jump ship, I felt I had the necessary skills and had made some useful contacts. The first of these was the grand old firm of Meccano, producer of the original build-your-dream-machine kits of basic slotted steel strips, angles, nuts, bolts and motors that every child with a creative bent longed to have for Christmas. Unfortunately, this was when the home computer age was just beginning and a short time later, when the computer game became all the rage, Meccano Ltd went to the wall and, sadly, is no more, but that is another story.

Meccano was also the maker of the small, highly detailed range of models called Dinky Toys, which included not only a range of cars and aircraft, but also a tie-in with several film companies producing promotional models to go with whichever the was current prestige film of the time. One of these companies was 'Century 21', a company producing very lifelike and futuristic puppet films for TV and the big screen such as the *Thunderbirds*, *Captain Scarlet* and *Joe 90* series. My task here was first to produce the original designs in prototype form, and then the patterns for the production of many of the promotional models that have become collectors' items by the followers of this genre in later years. At this time, my work also included the production of some of the smaller film props for a subsidiary company, in both puppet size and full human size. This was necessary, as in some sequences, for example, Captain Scarlet would be seen holding a device, and then the camera would zoom into his hand to see his finger operate it. Of course, the device had to change from a miniature in the puppet's hand to a full-size device in a human hand.

The time it takes to create a prototype and/or a set of master patterns from which the production dies would be produced can be between a few days and several weeks. On the other hand, the time required to make the tools and have the product in the shops would require very many months, and thus a freelance model engineer could soon put himself out of work if he relied on a single company for his livelihood. So I moved on to Mettoy Playcraft, the manufacturers of the second major die-cast model toy car, the Corgi toy, and spent a further two years developing and producing prototypes and patterns for several of that company's models, also now considered to be collectors' pieces.

This period of toy development was to be a self-imposed apprenticeship in model engineering, in which a further two essential skills were learnt for my later life in building the miniatures illustrated in these pages. In working with film props, the first was how to recognize the essential character of what one is making, and, secondly, to incorporate that into the finished article using very rudimentary materials, but in the quickest possible time. One must bear in mind that even the most elaborate film prop or set may actually only be shot from one angle for one minute, but has to be so convincing that you believe you are looking at real life. The prop or set can be made to any scale, and from virtually any materials, depending only on how far away from the camera it will be used. This therefore affects the decisions with regard to how much or how little detail there should be. Leave out a vital element that one would expect to see, or make a detail slightly larger or smaller, and the whole effect will be lost. The important point here is 'what you would expect to see', which is not necessarily exactly what you are representing, or making exactly to scale. For example, a steel girder with rivets along its length would draw the eye to it if these were missing down to a very small scale, and leave a question mark in the mind that would distract it from the rest of the scene. Placing small dots where one would expect to see the rivets would sufficiently satisfy the eye so that it would allow the brain to accept the scene and move on. This is always provided that they are not 'out of scale', as this would have the same effect of distracting the eye.

I believe that it is an art as well as a craft to know instinctively what to include and what to leave out in all aspects of scale model making in general. Unless your aim is to reproduce every detail exactly to scale just for the sake of it, which, on anything less than a quarter scale for a model car, would not be practicable because of the lack of thickness of the sheet metal, then some form of licence has to be used. What form that licence takes would depend on what you wish to portray or achieve with the finished model.

M45 Lagonda, Blower Bentley and S-Type Invicta built without engine or chassis detail in one-twentieth scale.

MG J2 built without engine or chassis detail in one-twentieth scale.

Lessons learned from the work with Dinky and Corgi toys were mainly to do with looking at a subject, particularly a car, and mentally dissecting it into manageable parts that could then be made by hand or manufactured. The difference between the two is quite significant, as anything can be made by hand, provided unlimited time is available. To design a part for manufacture, and to make more identical pieces using a method such as casting, requires much more consideration to be given to the shape of the item, because certain restrictions are imposed depending on the process under consideration. (One could write a book on this alone!) This ability of knowing what is or is not possible from the manufacturing processes available, both old and new, is of incalculable value, particularly in my own field of automobile miniatures.

The start of car modelling as a profession came when I was commissioned by Lord Montagu of Beaulieu to contribute to the collections that he was having built for the then Montagu Motor Museum, later to be renamed the National Motor Museum, in Beaulieu, Hampshire, England. There were two model collections that had been started by another model-maker called Rex Hays. The first of these was to show the evolution of the sports car, and the second was a series of the World Champion GP car each year. The scale of the models had already been determined at one-twentieth, making the individual models about 6 to 8in (152–203mm) in length. These were to be curbside models with no engine or chassis detail. Rex Hays had already built about two dozen models for the collection when I came on the scene. As most of his models had wooden bodywork, there had been a problem with cracks developing in the paintwork. I had also, from the start, made my car bodies from hardwood, but had bonded them into a thin sheet metal shell that had first been hammered over a hardwood block, and so they did not suffer from the surface cracking of the paint finish. In all, I built twenty-one of the one-twentieth scale miniatures for the museum. On 6 December 1999, the National Motor Museum (NMM) put the model collections under the hammer of the renowned auction house Brooks in London. These early models were sold at twenty-one times the price that they had been built for twenty years earlier. This included a 1930 S-Type Invicta (without engine or chassis detail) which was originally priced at £150.

While building the NMM miniatures in the first few years as a professional model engineer, research for original data become a major preoccupation. I made a point of visiting each car personally to photograph it and take down sufficient data and dimensions to be able to draft a set of scale plans for the project. It soon transpired that there were very few, if any, general arrangement drawings available of cars of any sort, even less so of the particularly rare ones that were on the to-be-made list. Whilst some model makers do build models from photographs and book illustrations, I felt it necessary to see the whole car, remembering the awe-inspiring experience of standing on the deck of the *Cutty Sark* in Greenwich, London, when building sailing ship models. If you wish to build a lifelike miniature there is no substitute for actually seeing and experiencing the presence of your subject. This turned out to be a good decision, as not only did I get to see the cars, but also to meet the owners, who invariably asked if a second miniature could be made for them, while building the one for the Museum. It was not long before the request came for a more detailed miniature of slightly larger proportions, as the scale of one-twentieth was a little small for the full engine and chassis to be shown. I decided on the larger but unusual scale of one-fifteenth. This was the time when everything was turning metric, so I did not think it appropriate to use the more usual scales of one-sixteenth or one-eighteenth. To my delight several years later, I came across several original drawings by Ettore Bugatti for the Bugatti Type 41 chassis of 1930, drafted to the scale of one-fifteenth, so my choice of scale was vindicated.

As work progressed on the larger miniatures for private collectors, the orders from the NMM began to decline as they reviewed their ever diminishing space to show their ever increasing collection of cars. The final one-twentieth scale model for the collection was the 1975 World Championship 312 Ferrari of Niki Lauda. From then on, all the car miniatures have been created in the larger scale, with the exception of three, with full engine and chassis detail and for private collectors.

At the same time, articles on this work were appearing in print and several television programs were made on the miniatures and the workshop. This, together with three books on the techniques used (the first actually on ship modelling), meant that the name of Wingrove started to spread far and wide in connection with fine detail car miniatures. A career that is now three decades long was launched, and with the able assistance of Phyllis, my wife and 'life partner', we have created just over 220 pieces, at the last count, for collectors in Japan, the USA, Europe and the UK.

The Art of the Automobile

Art, it is said, 'is in the eye of the beholder', and in this day and age of piles of rubbish, unmade beds and pickled sharks and cows being declared as art, this is more true than ever. For some, the car is just a means of transport, but it has been with us in one form or another for over one hundred years, and it would be strange for man to keep recreating a certain object year after year, and not occasionally come up with a combination of elements of exceptional design that stands out from the crowd. This is more so with the car than with most other material items, not only because of the vast numbers made by innumerable manufacturers around the world, but also because they are, of necessity, all trying to look different. Each design has to be distinct from the previous one and from its competitors as it vies for our attention. Many designers try to incorporate an intangible element that they hope will reflect the image we would like to acquire, or which will indicate a certain lifestyle. We are enticed to part with large sums of cash in purchasing one, two or more creations consisting of a skin of sheet metal and glass, covering a mass of parts, which, in themselves, are characterless.

Although every car made has been created as a means of transport, the differing shapes emerge when one considers the manner and context in which each car has been designed. Whether it was built to carry an aging dowager in times gone by, or an upwardly mobile young person today, or just to be the fastest car on the block, these all contribute to the outline and overall shape of the car.

Furthermore, the style of the age and the country in which the car was conceived, together with the personality of the hand that designed it, make for its individuality, to the extent that it can start to take on a personality of its own. This is less so now though, I am sorry to say, as the omnipresent computer's characterless chips and electronic wizardry take hold of the design process. 'Classic' is a much overused adjective in this day of the mass media, but if we mean something that is outstanding for its time, which in terms of a car would not only relate to design but also to its performance, then there are undoubtedly a number of cars that would be entitled to be termed classics. A classic, however, is not necessarily a work of art. The 1929 4.5-litre supercharged Bentley is a classic car, but calling it a work of art would be debatable. On the other hand, the 1938 2.9 8C Mille Miglia Alfa Romeo, built incidentally with the same end in mind, that is, to win races, is, in my opinion, not only a classic car but also an outstanding work of automotive art. Art is not the product of an artist, art is what creates the artist. Alfa Romeo and its Carrossiers of Touring and Zagato in the 1930s would seem to have been blessed with artists of exceptional talent. The 2.9 8C and the earlier 2.3 8C series of cars built between 1931 and 1939 are perfection in their design and, incidentally, are also considered by many to be the greatest sports cars ever built.

I feel certain that in years to come art in the automobile will be recognized by historians and critics alike to be the most significant art form of the twentieth century, in expressing the spirit of the age. It is an object developed by man through an evolutionary process, which, at times, has produced designs so fine-tuned by outstanding talent that it epitomizes its purpose with a flare that can only be the work of a genius. For me, the high point of automotive art is the decade of the 1930s, and, as with the great painting, sculpture and music of previous centuries, some of the finest was centred in Italy.

But of course, automotive art does not only emanate from Italy. This is where 'art is in the eye of the beholder' truly comes into play. Both Phyllis and I also see the same art form in the work of Bugatti in France, along with Duesenberg and Cord in the USA, among others. Those with a broader knowledge will undoubtedly make other choices and extend the list. However many there are, one certainty is that as we start to move through the twenty-first century, examples of their work have now become immortal, and will be prized and admired as *objets d'art* by future generations for as long as the laws of metallurgy will allow.

These cars have become *objets d'art* because a few individuals have recognized their outstanding qualities and preserved them, in many cases without regard to the expense involved. In general, there appear to be three main categories: those preserved as museum pieces; those preserved to be used today; and those preserved to be recreated in the new owner's own image. Each has its critics, whether it be for letting the cars deteriorate on a museum floor by not being used, or for being put at risk on the racetrack by being used too vigorously, or for being painted in garish colours and having everything chrome-plated except for the tyres. I take this opportunity to offer a heartfelt vote of thanks to all who have contributed to the preservation of these masterpieces for whatever reason, as without their dedication, effort and money, and the skills of the mechanics and workshops employed by them, we would all be much the poorer.

Our experience has been that the higher the automotive art form, the more generous, open and friendly the custodians of these fabulous cars seem to be. It appears to matter not whether a car's estimated value is one or ten million dollars; a letter out of the blue from 6,000 miles away has, without fail, elicited an invitation to help ourselves with regard to photographing and collecting data from these vast investments, for which we are eternally grateful. Those old enough to remember it and to have visited William Harrah's Automobile Collection in Reno, Nevada, USA, may recall the elevated gantries in the roof that overlooked the vast array of over 1,600 classic cars, all roped off in long rows. For the general public, just to touch the rope would trigger a call from on high to get back and not touch the cars. However, the enthusiast who wanted to get a closer look had only to ask, and he would be given a free hand to engage in collecting data and furthering his research. On several occasions we had cars moved outside to be able to take better photographs – to these people, nothing was too much trouble. It was a great loss when William Harrah unexpectedly passed away and the Automobile Collection was sold off, mostly to private collectors, and in most cases, the cars were removed from public view. This being so, the cars are not lost to us forever. All will have gone to caring homes with ideal conditions, from where they are taken out from time to time, and shown to yet another younger generation, albeit for only a few days at a time.

So what is this elusive sensation that seems to form a presence around some cars and not others, something that appears to be more than all of its component parts? Having reflected on this for a long time, it could be said that there is something about design, date and/or colour, that brings back fond memories of times and experiences past to certain people, but this would suggest that it is one's memory which is prompting the presence around the subject. There is a large following for Ferraris, a make of car that I should admit, in hushed tones, has never quite appealed to me personally. However, back in 1975, one of the cars on the to-be-made list for the NMM Collection was a model of Niki Lauda's World Championship 312 Ferrari. I was invited into the Ferrari pits on a practice day and, between outings of the car on the racetrack at Silverstone, was allowed to collect my photos and dimensions for drafting a set of scale plans from which the model could be built. I spent most of the day there amid the noise, smells and enthusiasm of everything that is 'Ferrari'. I can understand the similar experiences that must come with owning and driving one of the roadsters, and there are many who would include some of these as automotive art. It also follows that just seeing the shape of some of these cars will spark the memories and excitement of times past. However, 'the art' has to be more than just touching the happy spot of a few individuals.

I gleaned much of the history of Alfa Romeo during the 1930s from reading about the exploits of the Bugatti cars of the same period. Therefore, when I met my first 2.3 8C Alfa Romeo, I was already in awe of it, and when its very enthusiastic owner (they all are) endeavoured to impress me with his 2.3 Alfa driving prowess, I was overwhelmed. This could be said to have stimulated my appreciation of what the 2.9 8C might do for me, when I encountered that for the first time. Its presence, personality and character were obvious right from the start, even in the insalubrious and darkened corner where I set eyes on my first example. It so happened that the engine was missing and consequently it sat at an ungainly angle, nose up. But just looking at those voluptuous curves, at the total, all-enveloping shape, this 1938 Mille Miglia 2.9 8C Alfa Romeo gave me the same feeling of enthusiasm and exhilaration that also comes from listening to the music of Verdi or being in the presence of a work by Michelangelo; to me, this has to be automotive art.

However, it is the Duesenberg that most illustrates the point for me that there is something indefinable within the design of some cars that is beyond comprehension. About ten years before leaving my employment in light engineering, when it had already become evident that a further fifty years as a machinist on the factory floor would not be something to look forward to, I decided to investigate the possibilities of the only occupation that had given me endless satisfaction, that of building models. Having had occasion to discuss the subject with a London dealer, he pointed out, among other things, that although there were many professional ship modellers about, car modellers were very thin on the ground. This was enough to start my investigations further as to exactly what a 'car' is. My experience to that point was of run-of-the-mill Austin, Morris, Standard and Rover cars that constituted the everyday mode of transport on the local roads – hardly a promising catalogue from which to make a life's work. After starting in the public library and progressing on to the local bookshops, it soon became obvious that there was next to nothing on car modelling, but plenty of glossy coffee table books illustrating cars from every age and country. All of the well-known British and European cars were there, as well as the more familiar classic American examples such as Packards and Cadillacs. One book in particular showed a single colour photograph of an SJ Duesenberg Convertible Victoria. I had never heard of this marque before and knew nothing of its history or the people who created it, but to my layman's eye it was perfection in design; it had character and charisma and I kept returning to it. This illustration turned out to be the spur that launched my career in model engineering, and car modelling in particular.

Research began immediately as I attempted to locate the owner of this car. The age of the computer and the Internet had not arrived yet, and it meant countless letters to anyone anywhere who might have information. So many were the replies that the research became diverted somewhat from finding this individual car owner, to the Duesenberg as a family of cars, and on to the people who had originally built them. We later joined the association of the Auburn Cord Duesenberg Club in America, of which many members are the present custodians of these cars. It was actually thirty years later that I eventually came face to face with the 1933 SJ Duesenberg Convertible Victoria that illustrated the book. The bodywork was by Rollston of New York, designed by Gordon M. Buehrig, then head of design at Duesenberg and a great friend of the Duesenberg brothers. By this time, we had met many of the present owners, several members of the current Duesenberg family, and had become firm friends with Gordon M. Buehrig himself. He always took a great interest in our work in general and in particular the miniatures that we built of his body designs on the Duesenberg, and later with regard to the 812 Cord, his particular masterpiece. My obsession was reconfirmed time and time again as I saw more of these cars, and learnt about them and the personalities associated with them. The interesting thing for me is that I, as a country boy from middle England, before the age of television, was hardly aware of the jazz age of 1930s America that was the culture that spawned the design of these cars. Yet, when I first came across the book, it stood out like a beacon among the two dozen other makes illustrated such as Rolls-Royce, Bentleys, Packards, Mercedes and Hispano Suiza, and so on.

One can ask, where exactly does this almost tangible aspect reside? Having recognized that there is something additional to the components of some cars, it has to be in the subtlety of the overall design. Change a line, a curve or a detail, and the magic can be lost, and this lesson is of the utmost importance when producing the car in miniature. How many photos of models are there that look like models rather than a picture of the car seen from a distance? If the model engineer has undertaken his work with his heart, mind and hands, then he has a chance of conveying the character and 'art' of the original.

The design itself will tell a great deal. The 2.9 Alfa Romeo Mille Miglia and Touring Spiders appear to be ageless, whilst the 40/50 Rolls-Royce clearly belongs to the early part of the previous century. Of the two, it is the Alfas that would not look out of place on the road today. The Rolls-Royce is certainly English and could not have been devised by a German or a Frenchman, and the Alfa Romeo can only be Italian. I feel sure the designer did not deliberately set out to make it look 'Italian' when he put his pencil to the paper for the first time, but his whole personality is in that design. Not only is it stamped as his, but it is also imbued with the glow that is to be found in Italian design in general. The design came from the heart, not a committee or a computer chip. As model engineers in the act of recreating this work, we have the opportunity of gaining insight into the mind of the original designer. Even the restorers of the full-size cars, who take them apart right down to the last nut and bolt, and then recut, replate, repaint and reassemble every component of the original, will not bring them as close to the master hand that first created it, as having to draft a detailed set of scale plans from the car for the miniature.

Visiting each car is essential, so that one can feel its presence, view it and experience it, then take photographs and make rough sketches to note down the dimensions. These will be several hundred in number, although to attempt an exact replica would necessitate many thousands. The aim in our work is always to try to capture the character of the original, the essence of the design. The detailing that we incorporate in the miniature is only there to that end; it is not detail for detail's sake. In recognizing that there is this imperceptible presence about the car, it would seem that in some way we become attuned to it. This will manifest itself first in the drafting of the plans, as, for example, in laying out the drawing for a wing. Several dimensions are taken from the actual car, such as the wheel centre to the rear of the wing, the wheel centre to the front of the wing, and the height at the front, rear and at its centre. Linking these five points together could be accomplished with countless varied curves, yet only one perfect line will be correct. By absorbing the presence of the car, it seems to become second nature to find this perfect line emanating from the pencil point as one proceeds with joining up the markers. Because of the inherent problems of perspective, even with a full side-on photograph, it is not possible to trace this perfect body or wing line. Before the miniature wing can be created, a set of hardwood patterns needs to be made, over which the sheet metal is hammered to form the wing shape. The hardwood pattern is carved according to the shape on the plans. However, there is no direct contact between the two-dimensional drawing on the plans and the three-dimensional hardwood pattern block, other than the eye of the model engineer. Here again a variety of shapes could emerge, but subconsciously, because the perception of the original is so profound, the correct shape more often than not emerges from the chisel's cutting edge. It is very hard to pin it down, but one can sense when it is correct and will know just when to stop.

The sheet metal is then worked over the wood pattern with a jeweller's repoussé hammer, with much heating and quenching in water to maintain the malleability of the metal. The wing may have to be made from several pieces of sheet metal to accommodate the complexity of the curves. These then have to be cut and shaped to fit together exactly, reheated to red heat and hard soldered together to form a single wing. The heating will distort the wing, and because we now have a three-dimensional thin metal shell, it is not able to be refitted to the master hardwood pattern. Here again it is a subconscious act influenced by the essence of the original shape that brings this to match it exactly. These three essentially unconnected stages – drawing, pattern and metal wing – are far

Scratch building produces more waste than car.

removed from the actual car, which is probably 9,000 miles away, yet they look correct. This must indicate that there is something other than the few photographs and measurements that were taken from the car which influences the outcome. This process applies to every part of creating the miniature, including all parts of the engine and chassis if that is also to be shown.

Unlike a painter in oils or watercolour, who can sketch the outlines of the subject at the start, adjust them to his or her liking, and then paint within them, or the sculptor who can mentally visualize the shape and proportions of the subject in the block of stone, the model engineer, to do justice to his subject, will have to incorporate the car's persona into every tiny part and it will not be until the last part is assembled that he will know if he has a model or a miniature in his hand. The difference is that the former is cold and dead, while the latter has the viewer thinking that he or she really is looking at the real car in miniature. To accomplish this, one will need to be on such a level with the subject that its impression, which has come from the original designer, is burnt into the psyche so as to be instinctively at the fingertips when needed. The style and design of the component parts of an Alfa Romeo engine are far removed from a those of a Bentley or Duesenberg engine. Any three comparable parts from each of these makes of car could not have been created by the same hand, and in making them you have to think and work with the mind of the original designer. Having said this, the other side of the coin is that two model engineers will not recreate the same part in the same way, since no two people see things the same way. What is illustrated here is essentially a Wingrove impression of the original car seen in miniature.

Whilst not all of the original subjects that we have built in miniature can be considered as automotive art, I would add to this 'List of Greats' the Weinberger Bugatti Royale and Bugatti Atlantic, also the 812 Cord and several of the 'J' and 'SJ' Duesenbergs (plus the 2.3 and 2.9 Alfa Romeos, I have already mentioned). However, the remaining subjects do have the necessary magnetism of appeal, they are of an age and show this to perfection. There are many other subjects from the world of the automobile that fit these criteria even for us; these are just the ones that we have been extremely lucky to have been commissioned to recreate in miniature.

After visiting the car, the building of the miniature will start with Phyllis drafting the plans from the data, photographs and impressions that we have brought back from it. The building of the miniature progresses from the ground up, starting with the wheels. This is because one's enthusiasm is at its highest at the start of any project. The wheels, which can be four or six per car (we usually build two or three miniatures of a given subject at one time), will probably average seventy spokes per wheel, times six (wheels), times three (cars). This would indicate up to 1,260 spokes per project. Each spoke requires two holes, that is, up to 2,520 holes, each just twelve-thousandths of an inch in diameter, which have to be precisely drilled around the outside diameter of both the rims and hubs. While we derive such great satisfaction from our work, as is to be expected there has to be at least one task that can tax the stamina of us both! This will be in drilling the spoke holes for me, and threading the spoking into the wire wheels for Phyllis.

The rims and hubs are made from round brass bar, machined on a lathe to the scale size, then mounted on a spigot (a holding device) in a dividing head on a precision drilling machine for drilling the spoke holes. This will space out the correct number and placement of each spoke hole precisely around the circumference, front and rear, of both hub and rim. The rim and hub are then mounted in a jig, a precision-made holding device that firmly holds the two parts in the correct position relative to each other. The outside edge of the wheel hub is set forward of the rim, to allow the front axle kingpin, on which the front wheels turn, to be as close as possible to the centreline of the wheel. The spoking jig will also hold the two parts in such a way that the holes in the rim and hub line up to provide the distinctive pattern of spoking that is individual to almost every car.

The spokes are of stainless steel, and when all are in place the wheels will be ready for their tyres. These are made from silicone rubber in moulds created for each subject and will be detailed with tread pattern and tyre wall markings noted from the originals on the actual car. Front and rear axles, springs and shock absorbers are all individually made by hand from round and/or flat brass or nickel-silver stock. Those parts that cannot be made within a single operation, which is most of them, are mentally broken down until the part can either be turned on a lathe, if it is round, or milled on a milling machine if flat, or held in a vice and filed to shape by hand. When a set of parts has been produced, for a front axle for example, they will be assembled with small pins or fine brass screws, and hard soldered together to form a single unit. Hard soldering means using a very hot flame to raise the temperature of the parts to about 800°C, at which point an alloy of silver is melted between these to fuse them together. This is used generally throughout the construction of the many hundreds of assemblies that form the miniature. In the final stages, particularly when attaching small parts to very complicated larger assemblies, soft soldering may also be used. Here, a soldering iron, or low-voltage electric current via carbon rods, raises the temperature of the parts to about 100°C, and an alloy of tin is melted in-between to fuse them together. This is only used in conjunction with a dowel pin actually holding and locating the parts, so that the soft solder, which does not have the strength of hard solder, prevents the assembly coming apart.

Next in line is the chassis frame. Firstly, the side members are machined to shape as flat plates on the milling machine, and then subjected to the flame to have a thin brass strip silver soldered to the top and bottom edge, to form the standard side-member 'U' section. Numerous and varied fittings, made on the lathe and/or fabricated by hand are then silver soldered to the inside of the side frames, so that the cross members can be attached. With these in place, we have a complete chassis frame. Spring shackles and attachment points for the shock absorbers, radiator, engine, transmission, firewall and body frame are made and added, followed by the wheels, axles and transmission, to form the rolling chassis. Almost all of these parts are fabricated from brass stock, small pieces at a time, and silver soldered together to create the larger and more elaborate assemblies.

The engines on the full-size cars, in most cases, will have been assembled from sets of large, intricately shaped aluminium alloy castings. Aluminium, unlike steel and the copper alloys of brass and nickel silver, is almost impossible to fabricate with solders such as the hard and soft varieties based on silver and tin. The aluminium solders that are available do not allow resoldering of parts without melting out the previous soldered joints, so making it impossible to fabricate a number of pieces through several operations to form a single complex shape. When silver solder is melted between two pieces of brass, the silver is alloyed with the brass so that the next time it is heated it requires a higher temperature to remelt that seam. This is most useful as it allows further parts to be silver soldered in place without disturbing those that went before. Aluminium is also difficult to cast in small shapes, as it has a coarse-grained texture that is very noticeable in fine detail and also weakens very thin castings.

Making the engine parts for the miniature from brass is not an option because the colour of the metal is yellow, and painting the brass casting with aluminium paint is also not an option since some parts may need to be polished. The solution is to make the main engine blocks from brass, but just 4 per cent oversize, then use these as master patterns to have the miniature engine parts cast in fine English pewter. The 4 per cent oversize of the master patterns is to allow for shrinkage in the casting process. The advantage of using fine English pewter for the main engine blocks is that even the very smallest detail will be reproduced from the master on to the castings. This pewter is almost 100 per cent tin, is a good colour match for aluminium, and can be lightly sandblasted to give a perfect sand-cast finish, or polished to a high degree to simulate polished aluminium. Engine and gearbox accessories will be hand made from nickel silver, aluminium or brass, depending on the part and its finished colour.

After the chassis has been fitted out with all its component parts, we move on to the sheet-metal work for the wings, bonnet and body. Before these can be made, however, we need a hardwood master pattern over which the metal can be formed. This will be carved from a close-grained fruitwood, in a number of parts that are dowelled and screwed together. The number of parts will be determined by the shape of the bodywork and how best to recreate this in sheet metal. The master pattern will be split so that each section can be used to produce individual wing or body panels. In the main, two metals are used to reproduce the wings and body parts. Thin sheet brass takes care of those that are flat or only slightly shaped, such as the bonnet, side doors, floors and the interior panels. Where compound shaping is called for, in the wings, rear of the body, and radiator shell, then thin copper sheet is used. The advantage of copper is that it can be heated to a cherry red and quenched in water (annealing), which makes the metal very soft and workable with a hammer. As the copper is formed and shaped it will 'work harden' to such an extent that it can crack if due care is not exercised. To avoid this, the panels are repeatedly annealed as and when required. Brass, being an alloy of copper and tin, can also be worked in this way, but it work-hardens much sooner because of the tin content, so it is used only for the parts of the bodywork that do not require a lot of shaping. Nickel-silver sheet, which is harder than brass, may also be used for parts where a particularly thin sheet is called for. If an aluminium finish is a feature of the bodywork, then it will be made from sheet aluminium and bonded to an undersheet of brass or copper with modern adhesives.

The wings and running board are completed first, usually from several panels trimmed and silver soldered together to match exactly the hardwood pattern shape. With these bolted to the chassis, the bonnet can be formed from brass sheet, which is assembled between the radiator shell and firewall with three piano-type hinges fabricated from stainless steel micro tubing. This is actually manufactured for the production of hypodermic needles, but is readily obtainable in 1m lengths in an assortment of sizes down to about fifteen-thousandths of an inch in diameter. Short lengths of the tubing are silver soldered to small plates of very thin nickel-silver sheet, which are then assembled in a jig on the milling machine. With a 3mm diameter end mill, slots are milled across each of the hinge plates at 6mm intervals. When these are removed from the jig and slotted together, a thin stainless steel wire is threaded through the centre to form a hinge pin. The lengths of hinge are then trimmed to size and soft soldered into place between the two side sections and two top sections of the car bonnet. Handles and catches are then made and fitted to complete the bonnet.

The car body presents the second large item of sheet metal work. Like the wings, panels are cut, annealed and then worked with the aid of a repoussé hammer. The rough shaping of each of the panels is undertaken on a steel block or anvil by working along the edge with the flat pane of the hammer to make the edge thinner and consequently longer, or by crimping the edge and hammering these down, which will shorten and thicken the edge. A combination of these two operations, together with hammering the centre of the plate with the ball of the hammer to dish it, is all that is required to form almost any shape needed. The hardwood master pattern is only used in the final stages of shaping the panels. Each piece of sheet copper or brass is formed in excess of its final shape, then hammered over the pattern to stretch it to the required form. In this way, damage to the surface of the wooden pattern is kept to a minimum. When all of the panels exactly fit the shapes required, each is trimmed to fit its neighbour and, where necessary, silver soldered together. These are then reworked with the hammer, cleaned up with abrasive paper and refitted over the master pattern to be burnished with the flat pane of the repoussé hammer to work-harden the surface.

With the body panels complete, flat brass strips of one-sixteenth and one-eighth thickness are machined and filed to shape to form the components of the body frame. This, on the full-size car, would be the equivalent of the ash frame, but on this scale, a wooden body frame would not be strong enough to fix the metal panels sufficiently well without the possibility of them coming apart at some future date. The frame is bolted to the chassis at selected places with up to six or eight small screws, after first laying down a ten- or twelve-thousandths of an inch layer of tape between the two surfaces. This is necessary to allow for the thickness of paint in the final assembly, otherwise the body would not fit, and also as a mask to prevent the body being soldered to the chassis. With the framework in place, the body panels are now fitted and soft soldered on, thus making a perfect fit of body to chassis. Doors are provided with frames and hinges and attached to the body, as are the inside panels. Doors are also fitted with working door catches. No attempt is made to emulate the working of the full-size door catch; the scale is too small to do this with any assurance that it could stand up to actually being operated without breakage by an untutored hand. However, the door handle and working latch will be to scale, and the door will click shut when closed. Floor, dashboard, steering and other controls are made and fitted, as are the seats, windscreen and mirrors. Head and rear lights, body trim, bumpers and the remaining accessories required to complete the miniature will all be fabricated by hand and fitted in place to complete the miniature.

This is always the most exciting period, for now will be the first time that we will have a chance to see the character of the car emerge in front of us. If we have it right it will be apparent, even at the bare metal stage. Here at last we see what all the very long hours over several months have been about; it is as if by magic that the miniature is born, several thousand tiny parts, made individually by hand, by eye and judgment alone, coming together for the first time and taking on the same personality that the original has some 9,000 miles away. The impression cast by the original is so strong that its influence must flow unconsciously out of the fingertips to be recreated in the miniature.

With the miniature now complete, it is taken apart piece by piece back to the basic components. The body is removed and stripped, all fittings having been either attached with small dowel pins and/or small screws just for this purpose. The chassis frame, axles, transmission, lamp steering, engine and gearbox, are all separated out and accessories detached. The purpose of this is to separate those parts requiring chrome or nickel plating from those that are to be painted or left in their natural finish. Each of the parts for electroplating is first cleaned and polished, before being attached to wires, about 18in long, with either soft solder or small screws and nuts, to form trees. These are presented to the platers, who attach each end of the wires to a frame for the actual plating process. With the exception of electroplating and casting the engine parts in English pewter, all of the work is undertaken by us in our own workshop. Casting and electroplating require expensive equipment and a specialist knowledge of its use. We may require casting to be made once in three years, and electroplating, which takes only an hour or so to complete, two or three times a year. The specialist knowledge can only be gleaned from a long experience of working with the process, so we have preferred to leave both processes to the experts. Neither the plating nor the casting, provided it is undertaken to our satisfaction, will influence the outcome of our work in capturing the character of the original subject.

While parts for chrome and nickel plating are at the platers, we turn to the painting. This starts with each piece being sanded smooth and any imperfections to the surface rectified. Each is then chemically cleaned and sandblasted to give a key for the paint. All the parts are spray painted with the original cellulose lacquer used on the full-size cars when they were new. The first coat is a modern two-part primer/catalyst etch primer, which is essential to have the paint form a permanent bond on to brass and copper. Several coats of grey cellulose primer are then applied, flatting down each with ever finer abrasive papers, followed by several coats of the finished colour, also subjected to very fine abrasive polishes, to achieve a high sheen, rather than a glass-type high gloss. As each has been so treated, it is carefully put to one side until the return of the plated parts.

The final assembly of all the finished parts can be the most nerve-racking of the whole creative process. Up to this point, anything can be remade, repaired or changed without a major setback in the overall building of the miniature. With each part (and there will be several hundred) now sporting its final finish of either polished chrome or polished paintwork, a too-tight fit here or a slip of a tool there can make for big problems as the work progresses. The miniature is now like a very complicated three-dimensional jigsaw puzzle, with each piece having its own rightful place between two or more adjacent parts, which can only be fitted at one particular time in the reassembly. To find that piece still on the workbench after the miniature is two-thirds built is my permanent nightmare at this final stage. The compensation is of course seeing the miniature come to life and contemplating the mystery of how it has arrived at this stage.

To see if it does have the life and character of the original, we make a point of taking the finished miniature into the garden or out into the Lincolnshire countryside to photograph it against a natural background. Using a 28mm lens attached to the camera to create a moderately wide angle, thus throwing the background a little further back, the miniature is placed on a small section of scale roadway made for the purpose, just 18in from the camera lens. The lens is then stopped down to give a maximum depth of field to produce a photograph with the foreground and most of the background in sufficiently sharp focus so as not to indicate the size of the miniature. If it has been built with inspiration then it will not give its true size away, so the viewer may think that he or she is looking at the full-size car. If not, then you will recognize what you see as just another model of an interesting automobile.

Throughout this work are a number of such photographs of many of our favourite subjects. Each has given endless hours of satisfaction in its creation. The viewer can decide while perusing them whether or not we have captured in miniature the personality and the art of some of the finest examples of precision craftsmanship on four wheels. For your interest there are just two colour illustrations showing full-size cars featured in this book – the remainder are miniatures of less than 18in (460mm) in overall length.

The Miniatures

Alfa Romeo P3

OPPOSITE: 1932 Alfa Romeo P3 with full engine and chassis detail in one-fifteenth scale with half-elliptical rear suspension.

THE SUBJECT OF THIS MINIATURE IS AN EXTREMELY INTERESTING CAR. NOT only was the 2.6-litre Alfa Romeo Monoposto, better known as the P3, the first European Grand Prix car to be designed and raced as a single-seater, with the driver seated in the centre of the chassis, but this particular car has chassis number B5001, making it the first of the first. As is the practice with Grand Prix cars even today, they are forever being modified to keep them competitive, and this is even more so with B5001 as it was on this chassis that Alfa Romeo undertook most of the development of the breed.

The earliest photographs show the car with a very non-typical Alfa radiator cowl consisting of a number of vertical bars set in an eight-sided frame. However, by 5 June 1932, its debut at the Italian Grand Prix at Monza, the radiator cowl had been replaced by the one we see today. As appeared to be the custom with Alfa Romeo when entering a new car for the first race with Tazio Nuvolari at the wheel, it came in first with an average speed for the five-hour race of just over 104mph (167km/h). This almost equalled the lap record for Monza, set in 1924 by the forerunner of the Monoposto, the Alfa Romeo P2.

Two other noticeable differences between its first appearance at Monza in 1932 and the present day are the wider body and the reversed quarter-elliptic springs for the rear axle. The former was modified as a result of a change in the rules governing the Grand Prix Formula at the start of the 1934 season, when it was stipulated that the body width could not be less than 33½in (850mm). The reversed quarter-elliptical springs first appeared in 1935 when Nuvolari drove a P3 so equipped in the Pau Grand Prix. By this time, Scuderia Ferrari had taken over the management of the racing Alfas with a team of drivers who happened to be well acquainted with the better handling qualities of one of the P3's arch-rivals, the Type 59 Bugatti. Peter Hull, in his excellent profile on the P3, suggests that it was perhaps at the instigation of these drivers, Nuvolari, Brivio and Dreyfosm that the Bugatti type rear springs be tried on the P3. Nuvolari in fact won the Pau GP with the car as modified. There was one other major modification made to the P3, although there is no record that B5001 was ever so treated. This was to cut off the front section of chassis frame just forward of the radiator mounting and fit a tubular front axle with Dubonnet independent suspension.

After the 1932 Monza win, B5001 was further successfully raced by Alfa Romeo and then Scuderia Ferrari, although after 1935 its particular history becomes slightly clouded. At the outbreak of war, a mechanic who wished to preserve the car managed to get it on board a freighter bound for Argentina. However, when it arrived the customs authorities impounded the car and it did not see the light of day for another twenty years. In 1960 the Argentine Customs held an auction and the car was sold to a local businessman for the equivalent of £12. After twenty years of neglect the car was in a sorry state, and in need of a complete

1932 Alfa Romeo P3 as originally raced.

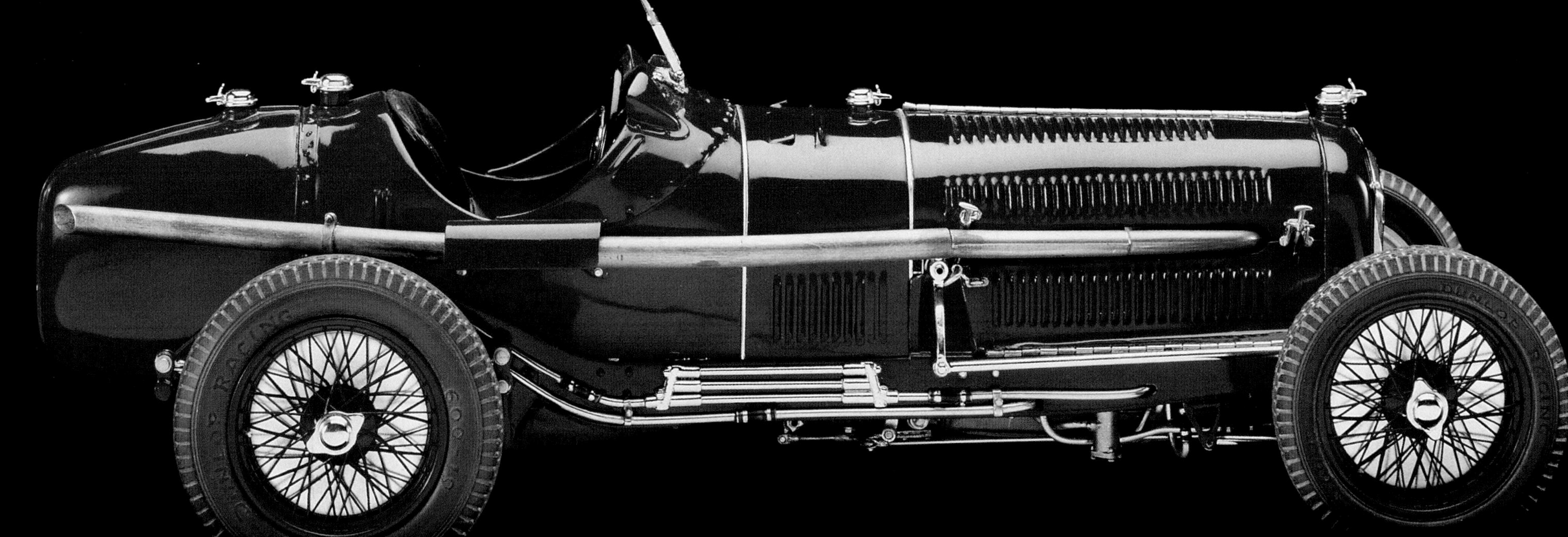

rebuild. The new owner and a colleague now set about taking the car apart, the idea being that each would undertake the restoration of particular items. However, much argument ensued as to who should do what, and so vehement became the conflict that the two former friends refused to talk to each other and neither would part with the pieces in his possession to allow the other to complete the car.

In the early 1970s, an Alfa enthusiast of the first order learned of the existence of pieces of a P3 in Argentina. After further extensive detective work he discovered to his great delight that he had found the lost original P3, or at least quite a lot of it, albeit in pieces scattered over many miles around Buenos Aires. After much wheeling and dealing, an incredible 95 per cent of the car was located and brought together in boxes and shipped to London to the safe hands of its present owner. The car was then painstakingly rebuilt to its 1935 specification, that is, wide body and reversed quarter-elliptic rear springs. In 1976, B5001 was back in her element, racing in the vintage sports car event at Silverstone.

It was my good luck to be invited on the scene to build a fully detailed miniature of the car soon after the pieces first arrived in London. I was able to photograph the car in several stages of reconstruction, which is invaluable if you wish to show full engine, gearbox and chassis detail. The plans were drafted for the model to a scale of one to fifteen in 1977 and the first six miniatures were completed in the late spring of 1979. In all, nine miniatures have now been built, three with quarter-elliptic rear springs, and six with the half-elliptic rear springs originally fitted to the car.

Although it is not our practice to keep a check on how many parts there are in a miniature, or how long it takes to make them, in these very early years I did make a record for this project. Had I kept to normal working hours (in those days a forty-four hour week), which I do not, preferring to work a twelve-hour day for seven days a week until the project is finished, it worked out that to complete the project would have taken about fifteen months, and in all about 14,000 pieces were fabricated to arrive at six complete cars. Thirty-two rough drawings, seventeen scale and 246 dimensional drawings were made as well as forty-one jigs and patterns. One major tool needed to be made, this being a louvre press, the reason being that 200 louvres of forty-one different widths are called for on the P3 and the old tool was just not up to the job. This necessitated designing and building a completely new machine tool, which I did out of one-quarter inch and five-sixteenths inch thick steel gauge plate.

OPPOSITE: 1932 Alfa Romeo P3 in one fifteenth scale showing the inlet side of the 2.6 litre 8C engine.

The new tool is comprised of two main parts, the first being a cam-operated press with the actual tool made of a hardened steel 'D'-shaped roller set in a housing. The second part is a movable table set on roller bearings. On the top of this table is mounted a hardened steel plate with grooves cut across it at regular intervals.

A hand wheel on the left of this allows each of these grooves to be placed precisely under the 'D'-shaped roller. A handle on the right traverses the table backwards and forwards under the roller between two adjustable stops to an amount equal to the width of the louvre required. These two adjustable stops act as profiled bars, so that if tapers or steps are cut on these bars a set of tapered or stepped louvres can be formed with the tool. Examples of both are found on the bonnet of the P3. A rectangular clamping plate is provided to hold the workpiece (thin brass sheet) on the grooved table. The roller is then brought down on to this by a large handle at the top of the press, until the sharp edge of the 'D' cuts through the workpiece. The cut and louvre shape so formed is then lengthened as required by moving the lever on the right. The cutting roller is then lifted, the table indexed to bring the next groove under the roller, which is then lowered to form the second louvre.

The Grand Prix cars of this period offer some fascinating subjects for modelling, for the art of the designer to get the maximum power and strength out of the minimum of materials is visible in every part of them and all this packaged in the minimum of space, in a shape that is almost always aesthetically pleasing.

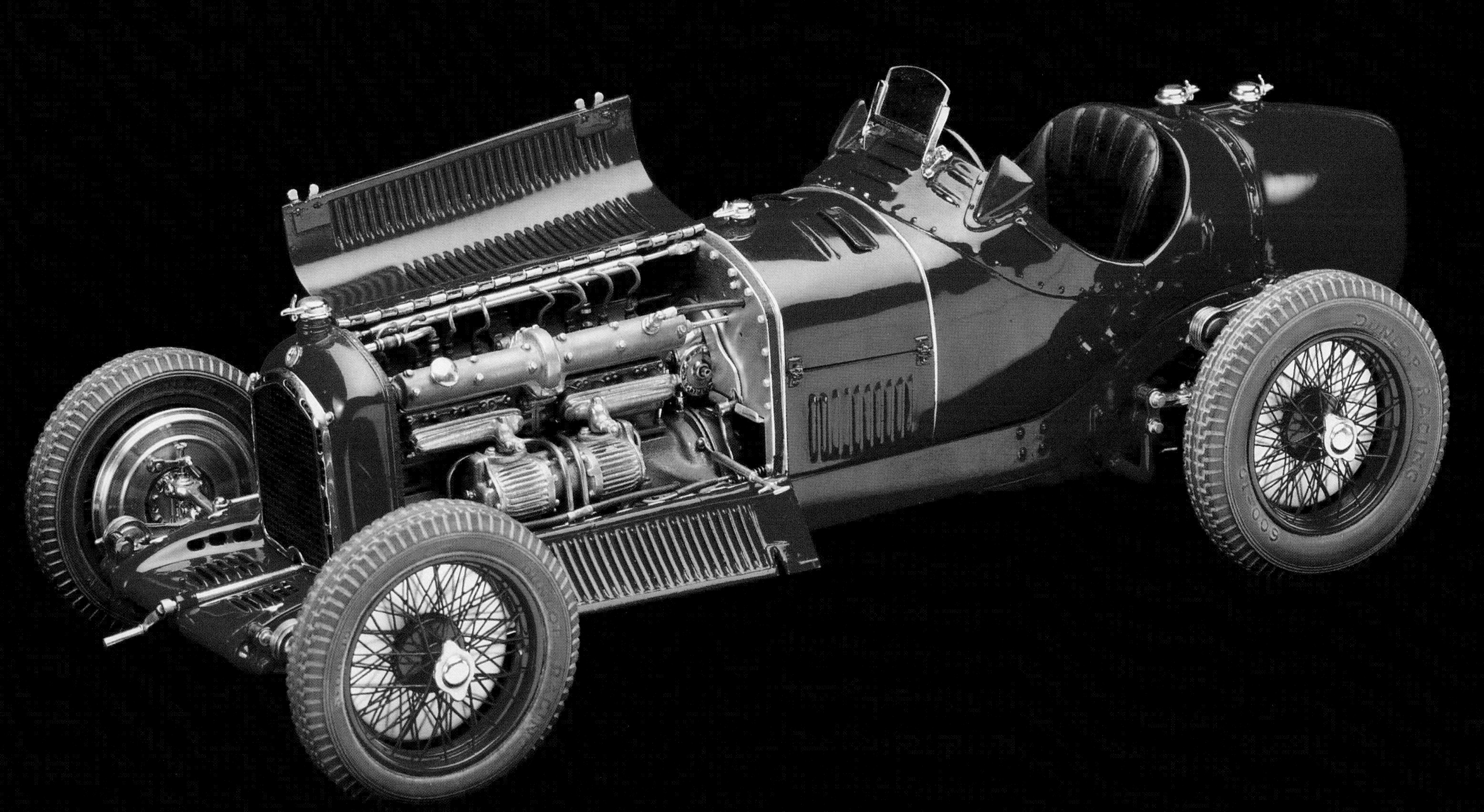

Alfa Romeo 2.3 8C

OPPOSITE: 1931 Alfa Romeo 2.3 8C with full engine and chassis detail in one-fifteenth scale.

THERE HAVE, OVER THE YEARS, BEEN A NUMBER OF CAR DESIGNS THAT TO my mind radiate movement, not I hasten to say, those monstrous creations of wings and fins from the American stylist's pen in the late 1950s, but designs that seem to grow when an engineer with artistic flair clothes his machine with the minimum cover for maximum effect. The Alfa Romeo 2.3 8C is one such machine. Whenever I see this car, whether on a photograph or in the flesh, it looks to be on the move, even while standing at the curb. Its long, low, sleek profile together with the flowing wing line gives it the air of a thoroughbred greyhound, its design is all movement – and this is just to look at the car. When one learns of its achievements in its heyday, one is even more impressed, for it toppled the Bugattis from their premier position on its introduction at the 1931 Targa Florio. It went on to keep Alfa Romeo in the forefront of motor racing for the next six years or so. The Alfa Romeo 2.3 8C wins include: Le Mans in 1931, 1932, 1933 and 1934, plus a second place in 1935; the Targa Florio in 1931, 1932 and 1933; and Mille Miglia in 1932, 1933 and 1934. The beauty of this machine is that it is not just skin deep – the engine and chassis are also a work of art, as was almost everything its designer Vittorio Jano created.

My introduction to the Alfa Romeo 2.3 8C was being chauffeured around in it by the owner, an Alfa enthusiast, who was determined to make an impression on me before I built the miniature. I delivered a finished model to him the following year, and placed on his desk a photo taken by Phyllis of me standing next to a car identical to his. He did not spot that he was looking at a photo of the miniature, and being very knowledgeable on Alfa Romeo in general and on his own rare short chassis Touring bodied car in particular, he became very excited that I had found another car identical to his in Lincolnshire that he had not heard of before. I left him to muse for a while, having contented myself that I must have achieved my goal since he thought he was looking at a real car, before putting his mind at rest.

The particular example that is the subject of this miniature (chassis No. 2111013) is unusual in that it is a 1931 car, one of the original prototypes, but fitted with an original 1932 body. It first appeared with a very rudimentary works body, two bucket seats and a slab tank at the rear. After its successful debut it was sent to the renowned Carrossier 'Touring' of Milan where the body that we now see was made and fitted. Not a great deal is known of the precise history of the car other than that it was one of the three works team cars, at the

Alfa Romeo 2.3 8C on the road.

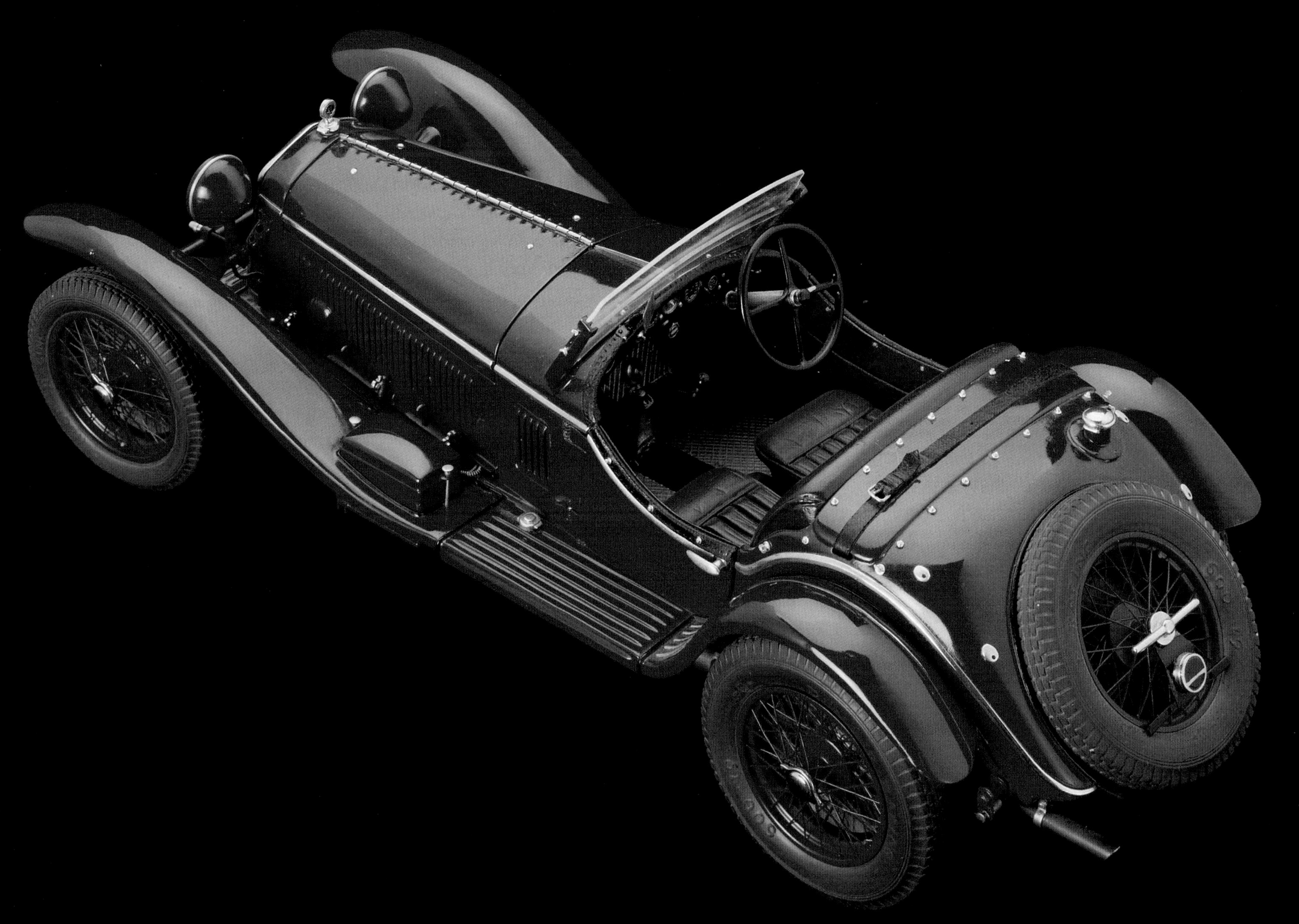

start of its life, so would have had drivers of the calibre of the legendary Tazio Nuvolari, Giuseppe Campari and Baconin Mario Umberto Borzacchini.

As subjects to reproduce in miniature, I find the thoroughbreds of this period most fascinating. It is only when you actually relive the design and building of a subject such as this that one can really appreciate the art and engineering that is in it, for when you start with a blank sheet of paper this is virtually what you are doing. It is one thing to handle and assemble a box of ready-made parts to form a complete full-size running car, when all the attention is focused on the internal workings of the finished project, with the senses attuned to the sounds, feeling and sensations of the car rather than the aesthetic appeal of the design. It is another to recreate a miniature where the concentration is, of necessity, solely on the look and design of each individual part, both when they are drawn in the scale working drawings and again when they are recreated 'in the round' in metal for fitting into the actual miniatures. A classic car design such as this, in my opinion, is as near to the beauties of nature as man is ever likely to get.

Phyllis hand-drafted four A3-size sheets of detailed scale drawings from the notes, dimensions and photographs collected on several visits to the Alfa, on some occasions when the engine and gearbox were out of the car for servicing. This is always a tremendous help when endeavouring to find where this or that control or pipe comes from or disappears to.

Seven miniatures have been built, to a scale of one to fifteen with full engine and chassis detail, built in three sittings of three models, followed by two and a then a further two models. Six of these went to collectors, with the seventh being intended for our own collection. However, another collector, the owner of several full-size Alfa Romeo cars as well as miniatures, somehow got to hear of the seventh 2.3 Alfa miniature residing with us. I received a phone call one evening to ask if we did have the spare miniature, and when I confirmed we did, he asked if we would sell it to him. On being told that we wished to keep this one for our own collection, he was clearly disappointed and terminated the conversation. A month later, he rang again and received the same reply, but not wishing to take 'No' for an answer, the phone call came each month for the next six months, until we finally agreed to let him have it. On meeting him again a year after this, we learnt that he kept it in his bathroom, because, he said, 'It made him feel happy first thing each morning, looking at it whilst shaving.' Such is the power of design.

To those that would wish to learn more about the ancestry and history of these cars, I would recommend Simon Moore's book, *The Legendary 2.3*.

OPPOSITE: 1932 Alfa Romeo 2.3 8C in one-fifteenth scale showing the inlet side of the 2.3-litre 8C engine.

Alfa Romeo 2.3 8C in the Lincolnshire countryside.

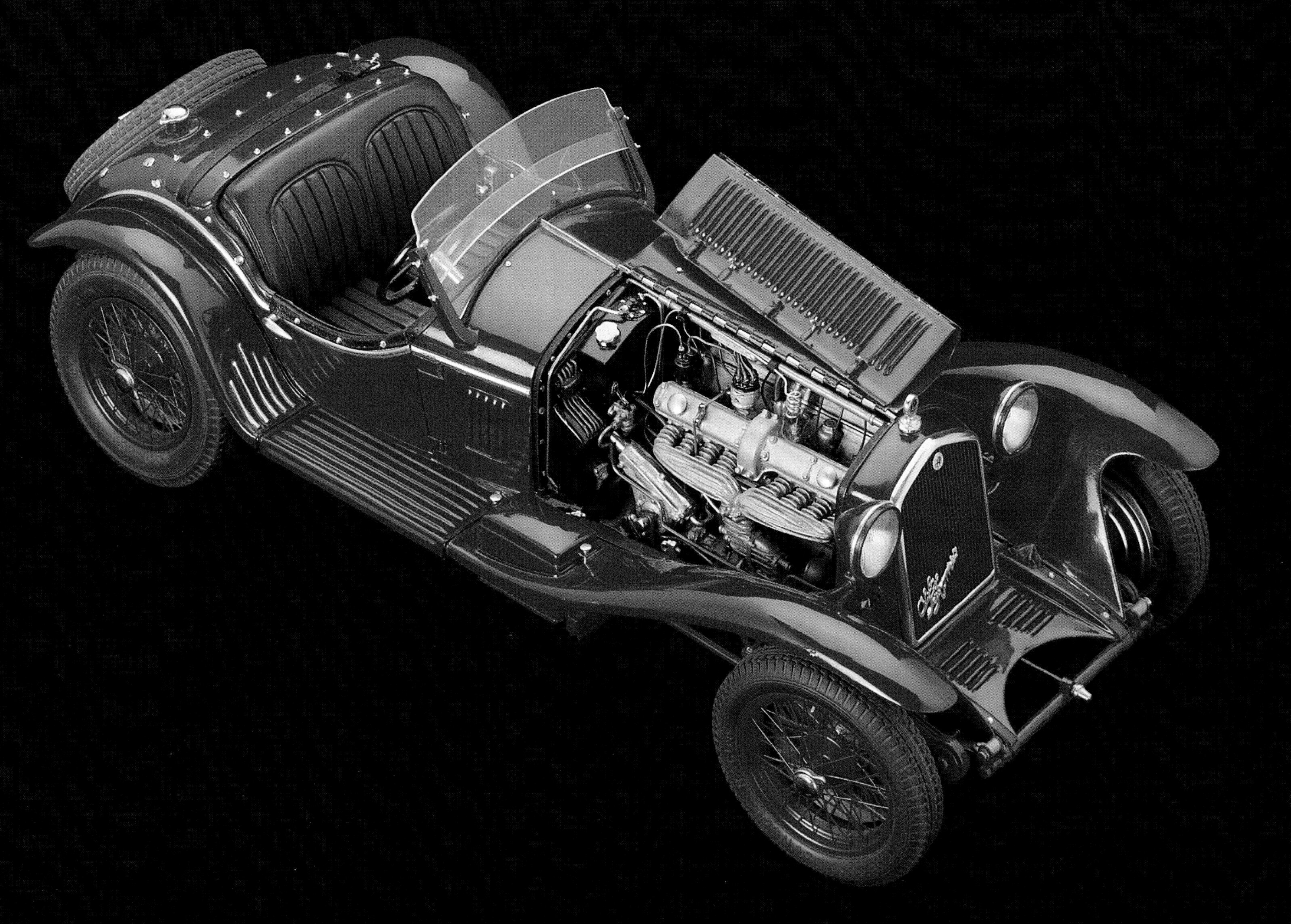

Alfa Romeo 2.9 8C

OPPOSITE: 1938 Alfa Romeo 2.9 8C Mille Miglia chassis in one-fifteenth scale.

My introduction to the Alfa Romeo 2.9 8C happened when I was on a visit to the American Brooks Stevens Classic Car Collection in Wisconsin in the late 1970s, my intention being to collect data from a pair of very fine classic Mercedes, a 1938 540K and a 1928 SS Sport Phaeton formally owned by the singer Al Jolsen. The Alfa was sitting forlornly against a back wall in a dark corner with its front end set up at an ungainly angle. Closer inspection revealed the reason for this to be that the engine was missing. Those voluptuous curves of wing line and rear-end were gorgeous. It was a bright red Alfa Romeo, of a line that only an Italian designer could conceive. Even sitting there at that ungainly angle, the car was magnificent. It soon became evident that this was not just a beautiful creation to be looked at and drooled over. The car (chassis No. 412030) was one of the four 2.9 Alfa Romeos that took part in the 1938 Mille Miglia race. Driven by Carlo Pintacuda, it finished a very close second to another 2.9, driven by Clemente Bionedetti.

I spent an extra day at the Collection to learn more about the car and collect as much data as I could from it whilst I had the chance. With our order books full of Bentleys, Bugattis and Duesenbergs, it was some eighteen years after the first accidental encounter with that Alfa Romeo 2.9 that we were eventually able to accept a commission to build one in miniature. The car in question was new to us and we had been sent just a single photo, a photograph that took our breath away. The car was a short chassis Alfa Romeo 2.9 Spider with bodywork by Touring of Milan (412014), the original prototype of this exceptional series of sports cars. The Superleggera two-seater sports body by Touring was the result of a special commission in 1937 by a Mr McClure Halley, an American Alfa Romeo enthusiast from New York. It differs in much of its detailing from the similarly styled cars that were to follow from the Touring studio. Most of the suspension and engine accessories are chrome-plated, the dashboard is of burr walnut with additional gauges to the standard 2.9 set, and the flash down each side of the bodywork is a wide, solid aluminium strip rather than the two narrow bands on most of the other cars. This flash, together with the petrol filler cap, hinges and windscreen pillars are all engraved with a very delicate diamond pattern.

Arrangements were made to visit the car and collect the necessary data for the plans. This was combined with much that we had gathered in the past, with regard to engine and chassis detail, from visits to several restoration shops. The 2.9-litre engine is, in fact, based on the 2.6-litre engine from the 1932 Alfa

Alfa Romeo 2.9 8C engine in one-fifteenth scale.

OPPOSITE: 1938 Alfa Romeo 2.9 8C Mille Miglia (No. 412030), with full engine and chassis detail in one-fifteenth scale.

The workbench at the start of the Alfa 2.9 project.

On the left are the hardwood patterns, the centre illustrates the basic sheet metal, and on the right the formed body and wing parts.

Underside of Mille Miglia 2.9 chassis.

The chassis and body together awaiting painting and plating.

Romeo P3, except that the Alfa 2.9 gearbox is integral with the rear axle and is replaced on the rear of the engine with a bell-type housing. It took Phyllis almost a year to complete a full set of chassis and engine drawings, together with plans for the Mille Miglia and Touring Spider bodywork, amounting to some sixty pages. By this time, we had progressed from a pencil and drawing board to an Apple Mac computer running Bentley Systems' MicroStation Mac, a very advanced yet easy to use CAD system, for drafting our plans.

These are drawn at full size from the dimensions taken off the actual parts. We were able to scan into the computer several technical drawings of components, such as independent suspension, chassis parts and engine accessories, and incorporate them into the general arrangement chassis plans. The move to a CAD system proved to be very opportune, as much of the detailing presented by this project would have taxed my ingenuity greatly. To begin with, the bonnet louvres were much smaller than could be handled by the louvre press that had initially been built to form the louvres for the Alfa Romeo P3. Secondly, to recreate the Touring Spider (412014), without the engraved pattern on its brightwork would not do full justice to its overall design and character.

The answer to both problems, and several others that manifested themselves later, came in the technique of etching, an ancient process used in many craft fields. I had made use of it in a small way in the past, but like casting and electroplating, although the basic process is a simple one, the technique is only learned from a long experience of working with it, and we did know of a local company that produced excellent results. Essentially, a drawing is created of a given size larger than the finished work, usually four times larger. This is then photographically reduced to actual size and printed on to the previously sensitized metal surface to be etched. The sensitized surface is then developed to harden the agent other than where a mark or line from the original drawing is reproduced. This is then washed away to reveal the bare metal where the mark was. If the metal is then subjected to an acid, it will etch (eat) into the surface

OPPOSITE: 1938 Alfa Romeo 2.9 8C in one-fifteenth scale, showing cockpit and engine detail.

and reproduce the design. Because the initial drawings are larger than the finished size, it is possible to put almost any amount of detail on to them that can, with the skill of the etcher, be reproducible on the finished surface.

The flashes on the sides of the Touring Spider are of aluminium, but as with this metal's casting and soldering it is very difficult to etch on the scale that we use, so nickel silver was decided upon as a suitable substitute. Drawings were produced on the computer to replicate the diamond pattern, which, on very close

A 2.9 Mille Miglia Alfa 8C on the road.

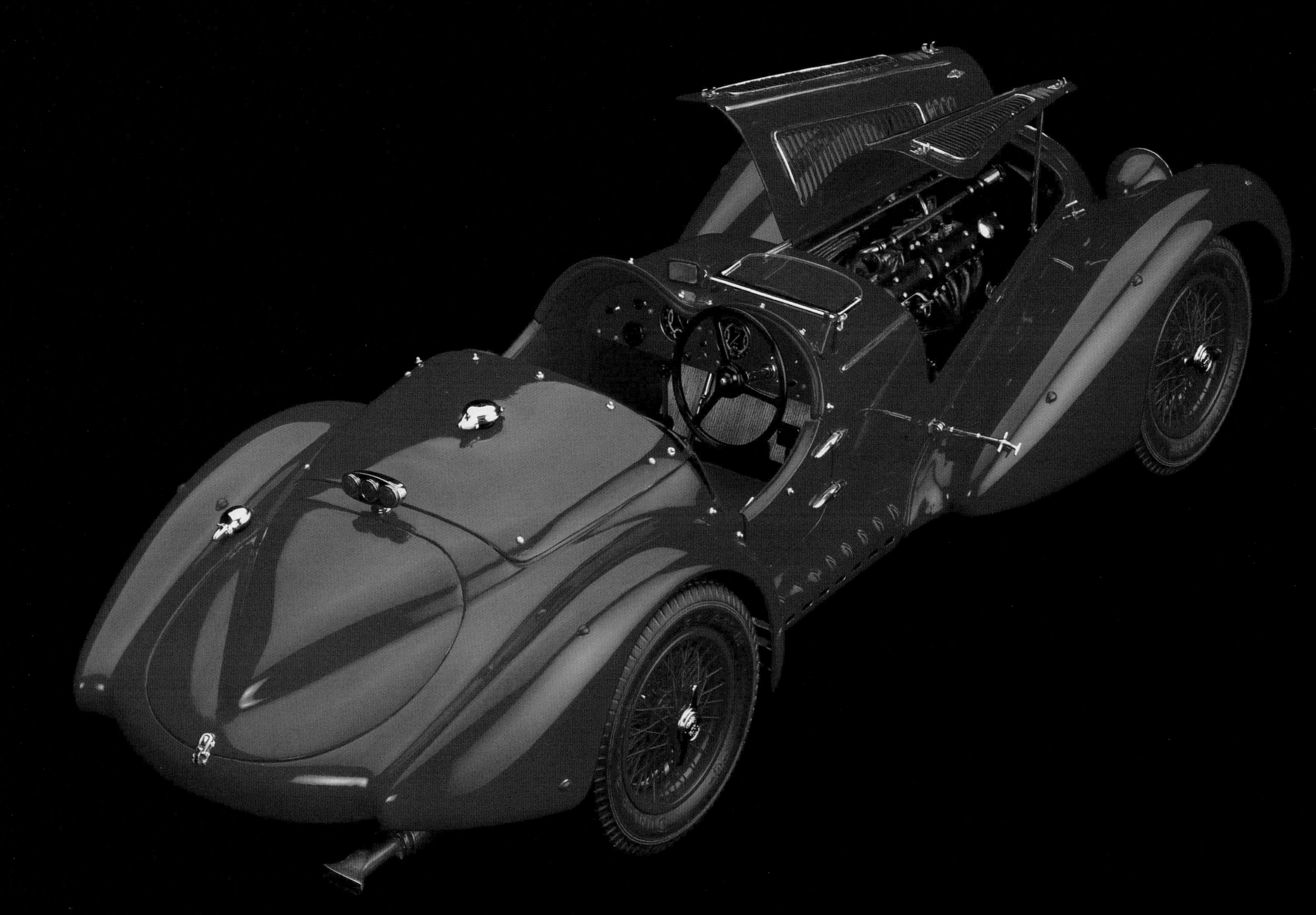

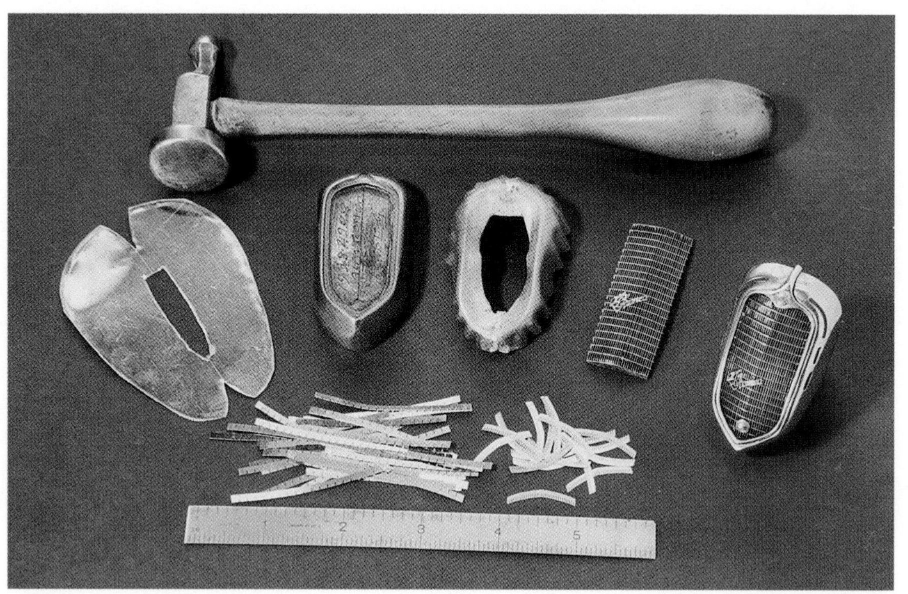

ABOVE LEFT: Three stages in making the radiator shell: sheet copper (master pattern); roughed-out shape (assembled grille); and finished shell. In foreground are the fifty slotted segments that form the grille.

ABOVE: 2.9 Touring Spider body panels and chassis.

LEFT: A pair of Touring Alfas on the bench with the hardwood body pattern in the background.

Complete miniature ready for paint and plating.

BELOW: Chassis and parts wired for chrome and nickel plating.

BELOW RIGHT: Chassis and body parts painted and assembled for the final fitting together.

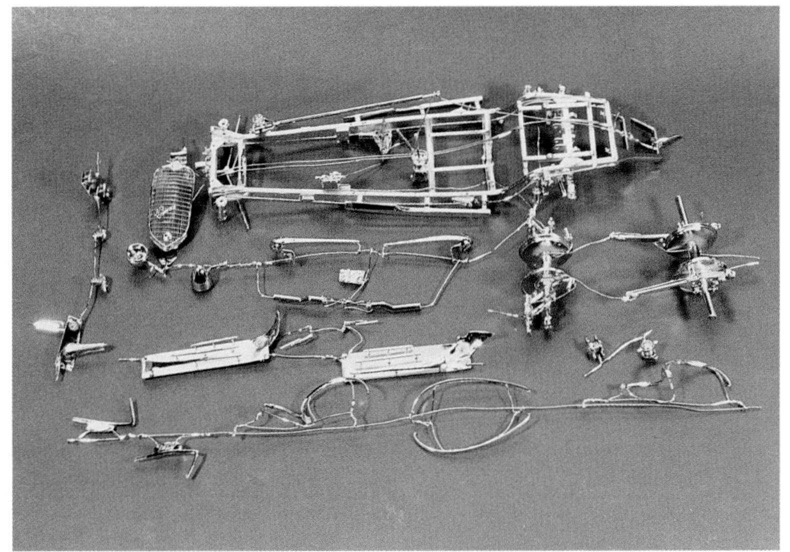

inspection, is actually in the form of wavy lines. It was necessary to generate 250,000 of these over an area of thin sheet nickel silver, sufficient to allow the sections for the body flash to be cut out. A similar technique was also used to reproduce, at scale size, the engine-turned finish on the 2.9 firewall, each swirl of which is just less than 1in (25mm) in diameter full size. The artwork consisted of five one-third circles drawn one within the other and precisely repeated over an area large enough from which the firewall could be made. This amounted to some 50,000 curved lines. Such is the power of the microchip over the hand of man. Etching was also used to create the small curved and slotted strips, that when assembled egg-box fashion reproduced the distinctive 2.9 Touring radiator grille exactly to scale.

It was, however, the set of very fine bonnet louvres of this particular car that had directed me towards the etching process in the first place. The technique proved to be very simple and stems from the initial drawings produced for the louvres. Basically, a louvre is drawn as two parallel lines joined together at each end with a quarter radius. In this case, the etching process cuts a line halfway through a thin metal sheet, and if etched from both sides at the same time, the acid will cut right through the thin sheet, but a cut from one side only can be used as a fold line to obtain a very sharp edge. If we now draw a louvre shape and etch it from both sides, we arrive at a louvre-shaped hole. Several of these stacked on top of each other will form a solid block with a louvre-shaped hole through it. If we now return to the original shape and leave only the line on the long side of the louvre to be cut through, while the two radii and the shorter line are only etched on one side to act as fold lines, we can place this over the block and by pressing the cut edge into the louvre-shaped hole, form a perfect louvre. The press took a couple of weeks to design and make; each new subject invariably requires additional tools to be made for it. To sum up, this technique only requires a few clicks of a mouse button and a visit to the etcher for an even more exact method of reproducing these essential elements of most cars of the 1930s.

OPPOSITE: 1938 Alfa Romeo 2.9 8C with Spider body by Touring, showing the engine and chassis detail in one-fifteenth scale.

One other feature of the Alfa 2.9 that did need much food for thought was how to recreate in miniature the very distinctive bonnet hinge. At first sight, this appears to be in one piece. Most bonnet hinges are made from two plates machined along one edge into short segments, formed into tubes, then linked together with a centre pin, about which the two parts can pivot. This bonnet hinge is made of just three open-sided tubes that run the full length of the bonnet. The central tube is curled under within itself, on both outside edges, in the

The Alfa Romeo 2.9 8C Touring Spider at home.

DUNLOP RACING

form of an almost closed 'C'. Around each, two other open-sided 'C'-formed tubes rotate. The secondary tubes are formed with a flat area extending out from one side of the 'C's, to which each of the two halves of the bonnet are riveted to allow the two sides of the bonnet to pivot around the two sides of the central tube. This is then attached to the bodywork at each end. Also, the central portion of the hinge on the Mille Miglia has a hood with a rounded cross section, while that of the Touring Spider is formed into a rounded triangular top cross section – and all of this in a scale diameter of just under one-sixteenth of an inch, and over a scale length of 3¼in (83mm). Giving the full lift to each side of the bonnet proved impossible to produce on this scale, because of the inherent weakness of a scale thickness of materials at these sizes. However, to go over scale for the diameter of the hinge was not an option on such a prominent feature, being a very visible and important part of the overall design aspect of the whole the car.

The problem was solved when I obtained some lengths of stainless steel tube of just under one-sixteenth of an inch in diameter, but with a wall thickness of just two-thousandths of an inch, which gave an inside diameter of fifty-five thousandths of an inch. Lengths of this were now formed into an oval cross section, while others were formed into a triangular cross section with generously rounded corners. One third of the diameter was then machined away to give an open-sided tube or cover, leaving a minute portion at each end still intact for attaching to the radiator cover and the firewall.

A normal type of piano hinge was now fabricated from stainless steel tube that was small enough to go inside the cover with very thin nickel-silver plates, attached to carry the bonnet. This was then assembled to form a normal style of hinge and placed inside of the larger cover from the underside, in such a way that the bonnet could be opened fully on both sides, yet the actual working part of the hinge was hidden from view when the bonnet is closed.

After completing the miniatures of chassis No. 412014 and No. 412030, we accepted two further commissions to build examples of chassis No. 412018, grey body with red flash, seats and wheels, and chassis No. 412019, with cream body, red flash and seats but with chrome wheels.

In all, nine Alfa Romeo 2.9 8C miniatures have been built to a scale of one to fifteen including two fully detailed chassis to date.

For those wishing to learn more about the history of the Alfa Romeo 2.9 8C, I can not do better than recommend the book by Simon Moore, *The Immortal 2.9*.

OPPOSITE: 1938 Alfa Romeo 2.9 8C with Spider body by Touring (No. 412014), with full engine and chassis detail in one-fifteenth scale.

Alfa Romeo 2.9 8C Touring Spider on the road.

ABOVE LEFT: Alfa 2.9 cockpit detail.

ABOVE: A pair of Alfa 2.9 chassis ready for the bodywork.

RIGHT: 1938 Alfa Romeo 2.9 8C Touring Spider (No. 412018).

LEFT: 1938 Alfa Romeo 2.9 8C Touring Spider (No. 412019).

BELOW: It is all a matter of scale.

4.5-litre Blower Bentley

OPPOSITE: 1929 4.5-litre short chassis Blower Bentley (No. HR3976), with full engine and chassis detail built in one-fifteenth scale.

Bentley Motors was in existence as an independent company for a mere twelve years, yet ask anyone to name a classic British sports car and Bentley is sure to be high on the list. Of all the racing Bentleys, the one that would come to mind first would undoubtedly be the thundering, fire-breathing, 4.5-litre Blower Bentley of 1929. Although, in its heyday, it never did win a race, it came very near to it in the 1930 French Grand Prix, when the great racing driver Sir Henry (Tim) Birkin drove a four-seater touring-bodied version, against a full field of first-rate GP cars, and finished second. The Blower Bentley has all the attributes and more that the enthusiast feels constitute a vintage sports car. It is big, powerful, complicated in the extreme, and above all produces sounds of authority, from the engine's resonant boom to the groans and wails of the gearbox.

There were just over 700 4.5-litre Bentleys built, but only fifty of them were originally fitted with the big-finned Villiers supercharger. Just four of those were prepared as fully fledged racing cars under the banner of the Hon. Dorothy Paget, a very wealthy lady who was exceedingly fond of fast cars and a friend of Birkin. The idea of fitting the supercharger to the 4.5-litre engine did not come from W. O. Bentley, for he considered it would 'pervert its design and corrupt the performance'. Later events were to prove him correct. The inspiration came from Birkin and was backed by the then financier of Bentley Motors, Woolf Barnato, one of the top racing drivers of his day and a multi-millionaire. Power increased by 80 per cent over the unblown 4.5-litre engine, but at the expense of reliability. Though new lap records were set time and time again, the cars frequently broke down and were unable to finish. By early 1931 the Bentley team was no more, and later that year the company was taken over by Rolls-Royce Motors. It is interesting to note in these times of ever rising oil prices and economy drives to reduce petrol consumption in cars, that when running at high speed, the supercharged Bentley consumes petrol at the rate of more than four litres (nearly a gallon) per minute.

My introduction to the Blower Bentley came very early on in my career, as it was one of the first cars on the Montagu Motor Museum list-to-be-built for the Collection. As was the practice that I established very early on, I was given a list of owners known to the museum who would be willing to allow me to visit their car, so that I could collect the data for drafting the model plans. There happened to be one on the south coast at Poole in Dorset. However, I was warned that this particular owner was a rather forbidding character (I was fairly young at the time and still somewhat green about the ears), and that if he did not take to you he would probably feign deafness and be uncooperative. I wrote to the owner to introduce myself and arrange a convenient time to visit his car to collect the photos and dimensions, and included several photos of my work. I received a very short and to the point reply, that I could come down when I liked, together with the comment that he thought the models looked all right, but the photography could be improved. I duly arrived on his doorstep in some trepidation to be confronted with, as appeared to me at the time, a giant of a man of very serious countenance. He took me around

1931 4.5-litre Blower Bentley (No. MS.3937).

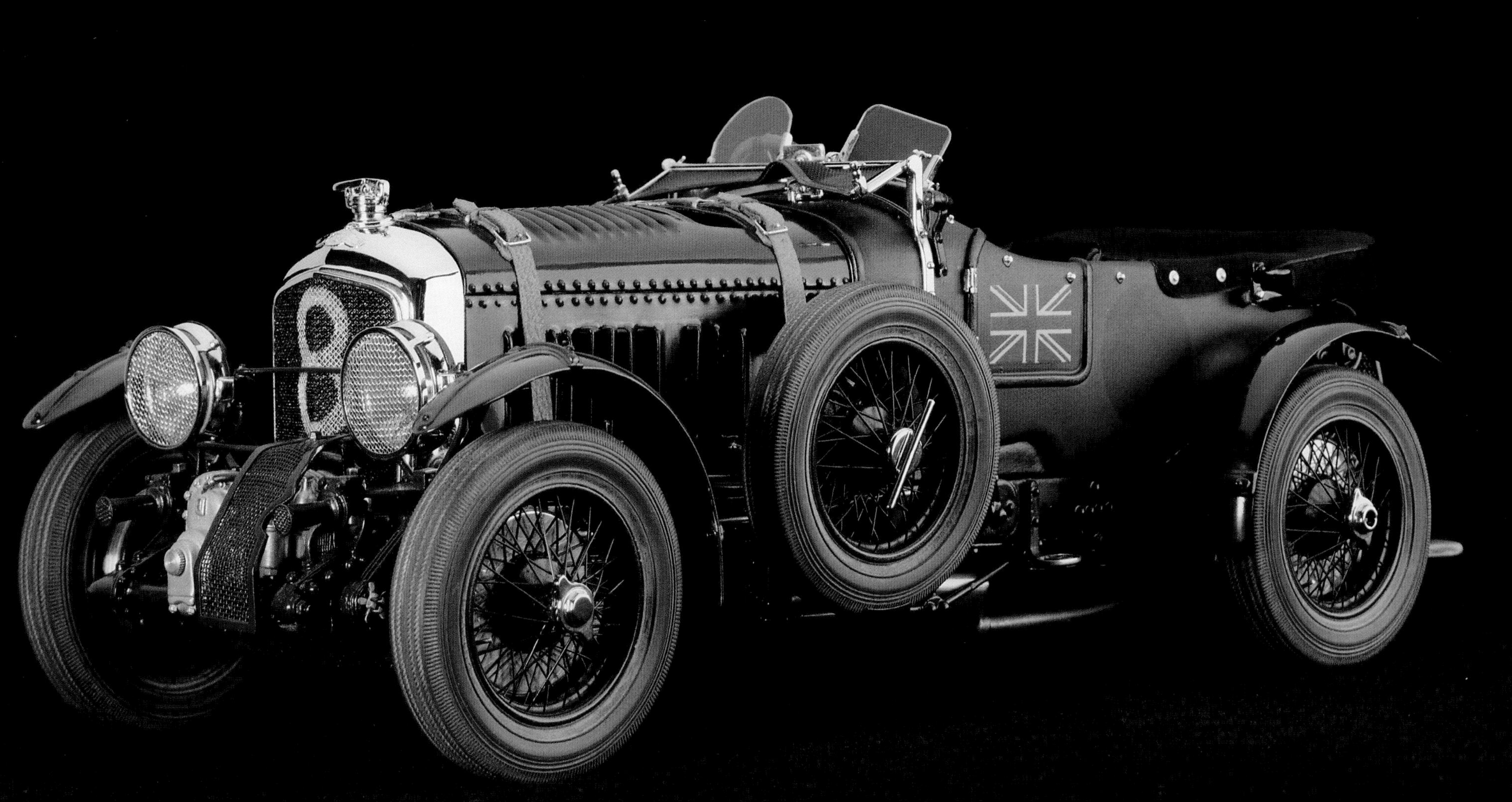

to a large garage at the side of his house and opened the door, telling me to wait outside while he disappeared into the dark interior. Moments later, a thunderous sound emanated from the interior, then stopped. After several more efforts were made to start the machine that resided within, a cloud of smoke come out at the final attempt, followed by a very large dark green open tourer 4.5-litre supercharged Bentley, with a very large man at the wheel who was red-faced and beaming from ear to ear. Such is the effect that some cars have on some people. The Blower Bentley may not be a work of automotive art, but it does have a presence like no other car that I know. I must have had the right expression on my face when he turned to me and asked what I thought of his pride and joy, because we soon became firm friends. Later, I built several models for him, including a model of his tugboat that he owned in Poole harbour and one of his Blower Bentley. The car was a particularly significant one, in that it was the first of the four Birkin racing team cars. It was fitted with a Vanden Plas four-seater touring body on a long chassis (chassis No. HB.3404). Three models of this car were built in one-twentieth scale without engine or underbody detail.

My second encounter with the Blower Bentley came about four years later, when a collector in middle England with a number of outstanding cars asked if we would produce miniatures of several of them. Among these was the number four of the four Birkin team cars (chassis No. HR.3976), also with a Vanden Plas touring body, but built on a short chassis. The engine on this car differs from all the others that I have seen in that it is fitted with a larger flat sump with finned sides. In all, six miniatures have been built, all with full engine and chassis detail, to a scale of one to fifteen.

Ten years on, and we are back again with the subject, but this time with chassis No. MS.3937, a long chassis Vanden Plas tourer that originally belonged to Amherst Villiers, the creator of the supercharger fitted to all Blower Bentleys. Apart from the different chassis length, all are quite similar, differing only in small details, such as the shape of the wings and the fitting out of the dashboard clocks. Three miniatures have been built of this car, all with full engine and chassis detail and to a scale of one to fifteen.

OPPOSITE: 1930 4.5-litre Blower Bentley (No. SM.3939), with body by Gurney Nutting, with full engine and chassis detail built in one-fifteenth scale.

Then in the mid 1990s came a call from 5,000 miles away for a miniature of a very different Blower Bentley. This was a 1930 special order for Woolf Barnato with a body by Gurney Nutting of London (chassis No. SM.3939). I do not consider this to be a very attractive design and it does not have the charisma of the Blower Bentley with a four-seater touring body being used as a racing car. However, it is a very purposeful and uncompromising design, apparently well in keeping with the character of its original owner, and I do like those way-out rear wings – very hard luck on the driver following on a typical wet and muddy English country lane! Just two models have been built, both with full engine and chassis detail, to a scale of one to fifteen.

1930 4.5-litre Gurney Nutting Blower Bentley in an English country setting.

GK 6661

OPPOSITE: 1930 4.5-litre Blower Bentley (No. SM.3939), with full engine and chassis detail built in one-fifteenth scale.

LEFT: Complete miniature ready for stripping down.

BELOW LEFT: Disassembled to basic parts for painting and plating.

BELOW: Blower Bentley engine detail.

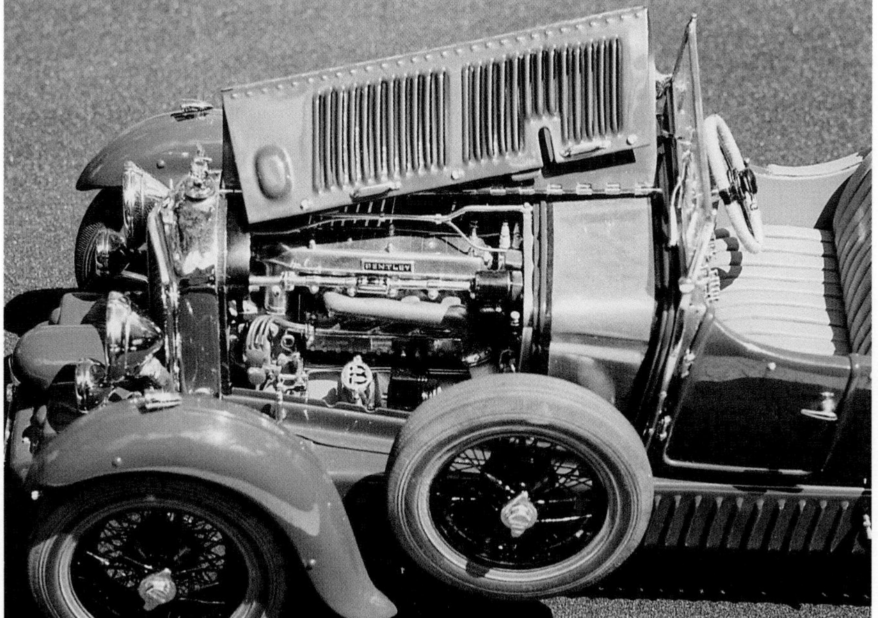

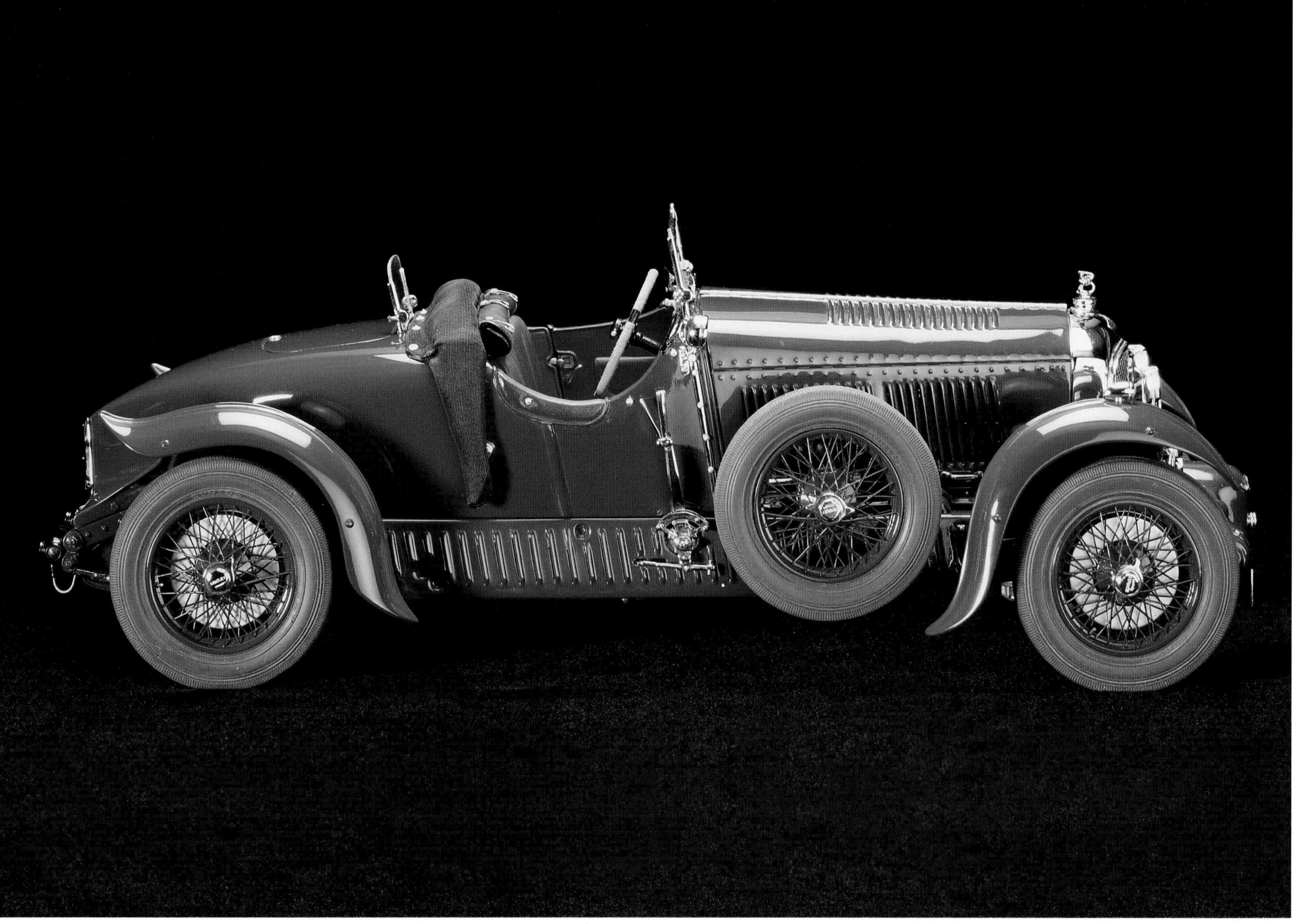

Bugatti Type 41 Royale by Weinberger

OPPOSITE: 1931 Bugatti Type 41 with body by Weinberger, built with full engine and chassis detail in one-fifteenth scale.

It was in the autumn of 1978, on a visit to the Henry Ford Museum in Dearborn, USA, that I first saw the Weinberger Bugatti Royale. I had gone there to collect data and photographs of the ex-Walter Chrysler's Chrysler Imperial of 1932, which is of a style and age that I find very attractive, with the aim of producing a set of detailed plans. The transport section in this complex is a particularly good one, and should you happen to be an addict like myself for the exotic machinery of this period, then you had better enter those hallowed halls with blinkers on, particularly if you aim to go there to work. As often happened in these circumstances, my eye started to wander and I soon spotted, not too far distant from the Chrysler, an enormous – large is but a small word in this context – white monster of an automobile. I had, of course, read about Bugatti Royales, but this was the first one I had seen in the flesh. So impressed did I become that I rearranged a very tight schedule of flights that encompassed London and Los Angeles plus several points in between, to spend an extra couple of days there to collect all the data I could on this, the Weinberger Bugatti Royale.

I do consider Ettore Bugatti to have been as much an artist as an engineer, and with the help of Ludwig Weinberger Jr's fabulous bodywork, regard this as their combined masterpiece. The Type 41 Bugatti has to be the most impractical car ever built, at 20ft (6m) long, 7ft (2m) of which form the bonnet. It is 3½ tons (3,556kg) in weight, with a 12-litre engine, a supposed top speed of 120mph (193km/h), and unassisted cable brakes to try to stop it. A friend who drove one of the two examples from the Harrah's Collection back in the 1970s recounted that after getting over the feeling of driving the Sistine Chapel, it really handled more like a truck. However, as a work of automotive art, it is hard to beat, but one needs to see it as it was at its inception (as represented by the miniature) and not as it is today. If ever there was the idea of a total design, it is this one; change the colour scheme and it is completely lost. I had often wondered, after seeing the car for the first time, why there should have been white rubber on the running board, but this turns out to be the key to the whole design. At present, the body, bonnet and wings are white and the yellow moulding and wing line a very dark green, together with the hood and trunk. This makes for a very short, stubby design with a vertical door, and no shape to the wings as this is lost in the shadows. In contrast, when the bonnet, body, trunk and wings are painted black, we have a very long, low design, enhanced by the black door panel which is now horizontal, and trapped between the yellow moulding at the top and white rubber beneath. This is further enhanced by the light fabric hood and the yellow wing moulding to bring out that magnificent and ever-so-long sweeping wing line. The headlamp supports were originally also painted black, to show off,

Weinberger Bugatti Royale at home.

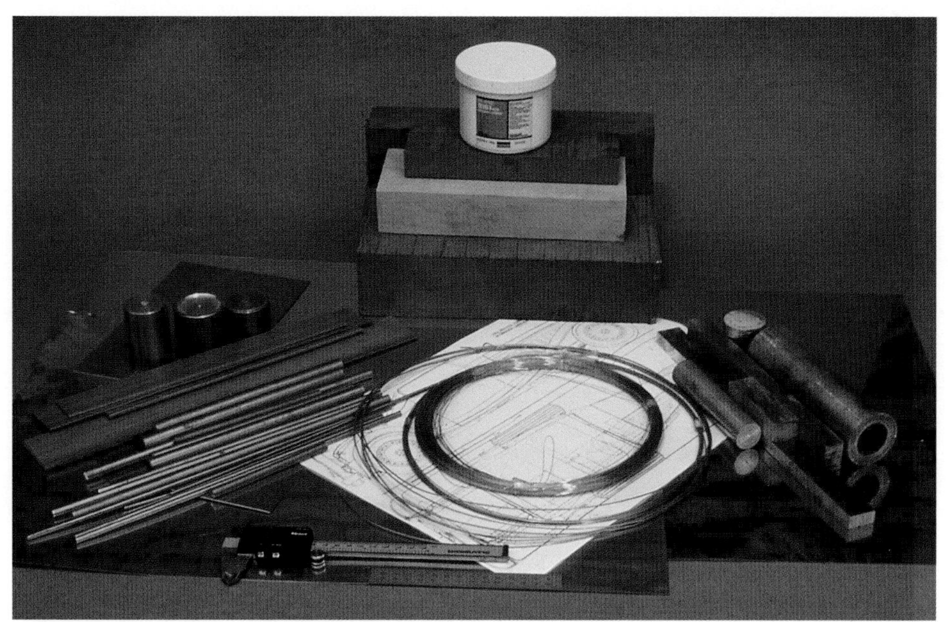
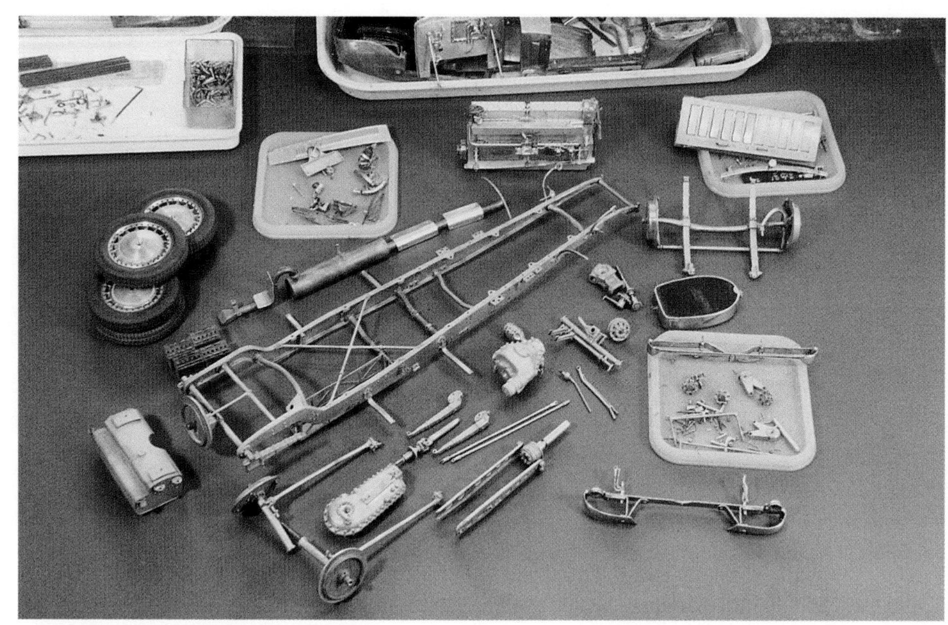
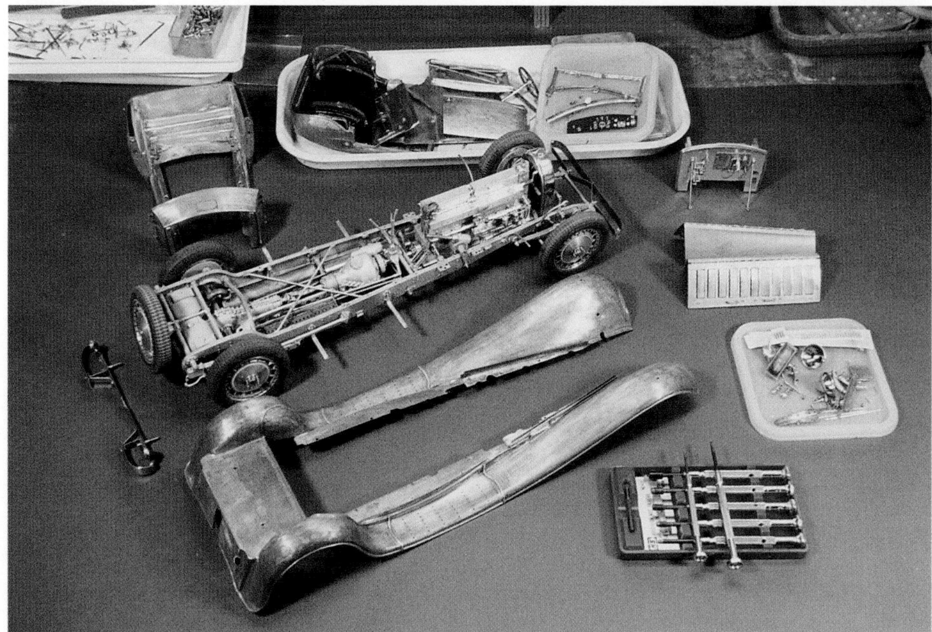

BUGATTI

OPPOSITE PAGE:
TOP LEFT: Scratch building from basic materials.
TOP RIGHT: Chassis parts ready for assembly.
BOTTOM LEFT: Chassis complete and ready for the wings.
BOTTOM RIGHT: Bugatti Type 41 engine.

THIS PAGE:
RIGHT: Chassis and wings and bonnet ready for the body to be fitted.
BELOW: Complete and ready for paint and plating.

unhindered, that beautiful Bugatti radiator. All this shows the complete mastery of the total design. Today, the headlight supports and additional driving lights are chrome-plated and this hides the distinctive shape of the Bugatti radiator.

There were six Bugatti Royales built, starting in 1927, and eleven bodies of varying styles and designs were fitted between them. I should say at this point that the number has since grown to at least eight cars, with the addition of a recreated (from largely original parts) Esders two-seater, and a totally new replica of the Coupé Napoleon. Of the six originals, only two were actually sold to paying customers who kept and used them – the stunning Park Ward Limousine (chassis No. 41131), built for Captain C.W. Foster, and the Cabriolet by Weinberger (No. 41121) built for Dr J. Fuchs. In attempting to recreate the 'Art of the Automobile' in a car such as this, there is no substitute to knowing exactly what you are looking at, which means researching it in full, right back to its original designer and owner if possible. It has been my experience with research in general that someone, somewhere will have just the piece of information that you are looking for, and is only too delighted to find a willing ear that is interested in the same subject.

The car had been extensively rebuilt in the 1950s by Charles Chayne, a vice president of General Motors at the time, and having been given a copy of a letter by him listing the changes, I started a research project that seems never to have stopped. Very early on, I had the great good fortune to make contact with Ludwig Weinberger Jr, the designer and builder of the cabriolet body, just two years before he passed away. At the time, he was actually drafting a second set of Royale body plans for a client, the first having been lost in the 1939–45 war. I learnt then that this was his very first project as a young man of twenty-two years, when joining the design office of his father's company in Munich, which, at the time, specialized in building custom coachwork for the top European car makers. It also happened to be the favourite of all his designs and he was most interested in our project of recreating it in miniature to its original specification. I sent to him copies of all the photographs that we had taken of the car in its present state and asked

OPPOSITE: 1931 Bugatti Type 41 fully detailed chassis in one-fifteenth scale (note the ivory steering wheel).

him to comment on any changes that had been made since. These were duly returned with many notes, colour samples and a small piece of the original Hungarian pigskin used for the interior, that he had kept in his desk since 1932. Also enclosed were copies of four photos that Dr Fuchs had taken of the car on the day that he took delivery. As the saying goes, the more one looks, the more one will find, which is enormous encouragement to continue to look even further.

Among the notes were details about the dashboard being originally of mottled aluminium and the steering wheel rim of ivory. Currently, the dashboard is painted black, but it does contain control knobs made from ivory, and the gear change knob is ivory too. In the notes from Mr Chayne, he mentioned that the steering wheel had fallen apart when he got the car and he had to replace it with a temporary one to get it home, after it had mouldered in the open through seven New York winters. The first two models were almost complete when we discovered a long-lost album of photographs in a very dusty archive, many of which had been taken by Mr Chayne or a friend, at the time he acquired the car. In the album were a couple of photos that showed the dashboard and steering wheel looking as though they had been of polished wood in better days. The boss was missing from the wheel, and so this could have been the replacement. However, there was also a photo taken by him in 1937 at the Roosevelt Speedway, Long Island, NY. This was significant in that it shows the driver's side of the car with the driver's window down, revealing a polished wood-rimmed steering wheel. From this we concluded for certain that the dash and steering wheel were both originally of polished wood. In view of its travels, it would seem most unlikely that these would have been changed and our conclusion was that Herr Weinberger must have suffered a lapse of memory. Unfortunately, by the time we had this indisputable evidence to hand, we had already built the first three miniatures, with aluminium and ivory

Detail of the ivory steering wheel and aluminium dashboard.

detailing. The five further examples plus one chassis, that have since been produced, are complete with polished wood dashboards and steering-wheel rims.

The miniatures were built following the usual pattern, except for the engine and wheels. Each miniature 12-litre, straight-eight Bugatti Royale engine has been machined from eleven blocks of rectangular aluminium and bolted together with concealed screws. It is fully detailed externally with accessories machined and fabricated from nickel silver. The actual wheels on the full-size car are a masterpiece of aluminium casting for any period, but especially so for 1927. They are double finned, with the first set around the circumference in the usual fashion. The second row is at an angle across the first and set left- and right-handed, so that at speed they act as fans to direct an airflow across the brake drums. The scale size of the detail is about as small as one can go with aluminium casting without them breaking up during machining, so I produced patterns for

OPPOSITE: Firewall and engine detail of the Weinberger Bugatti Royale in one-fifteenth scale.

the double-finned part of the wheels, left- and right-handed. These were then investment-cast in aluminium, turned and bored on the lathe and fitted with a front disc and rim of an aluminium alloy for added strength and to eliminate the problem of porosity where polished surfaces are called for. Each is also fitted with the ring of square-headed bolt heads as on the original.

Seeing cars such as this in museums, I have often wondered what story they could tell, and others must have had similar ideas when one considers big-screen films on this very subject, such as *The Yellow Rolls-Royce*. The following story could make an even better screenplay if anyone is looking for such a subject.

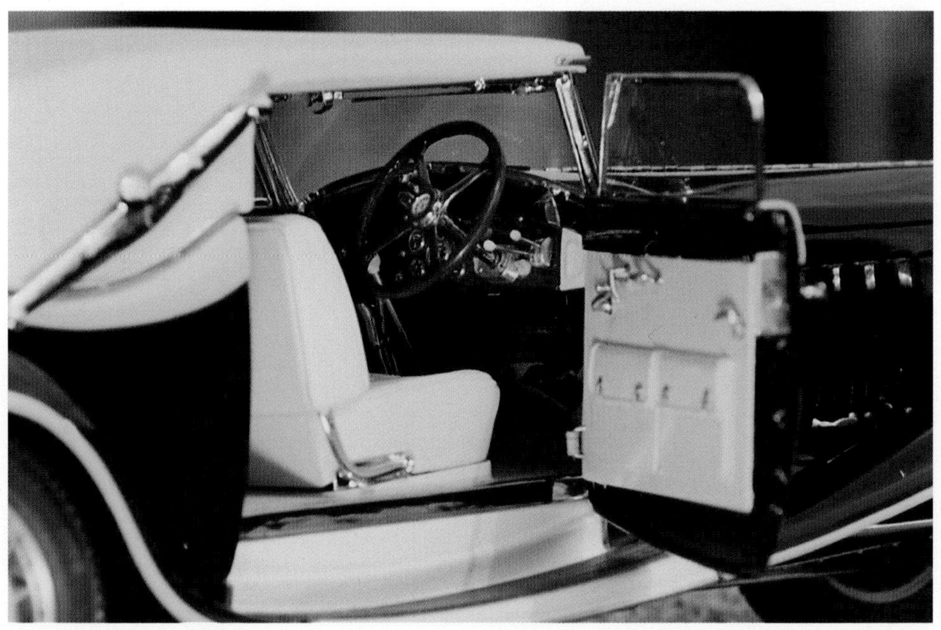

Detail of the wood-trimmed steering wheel and dashboard.

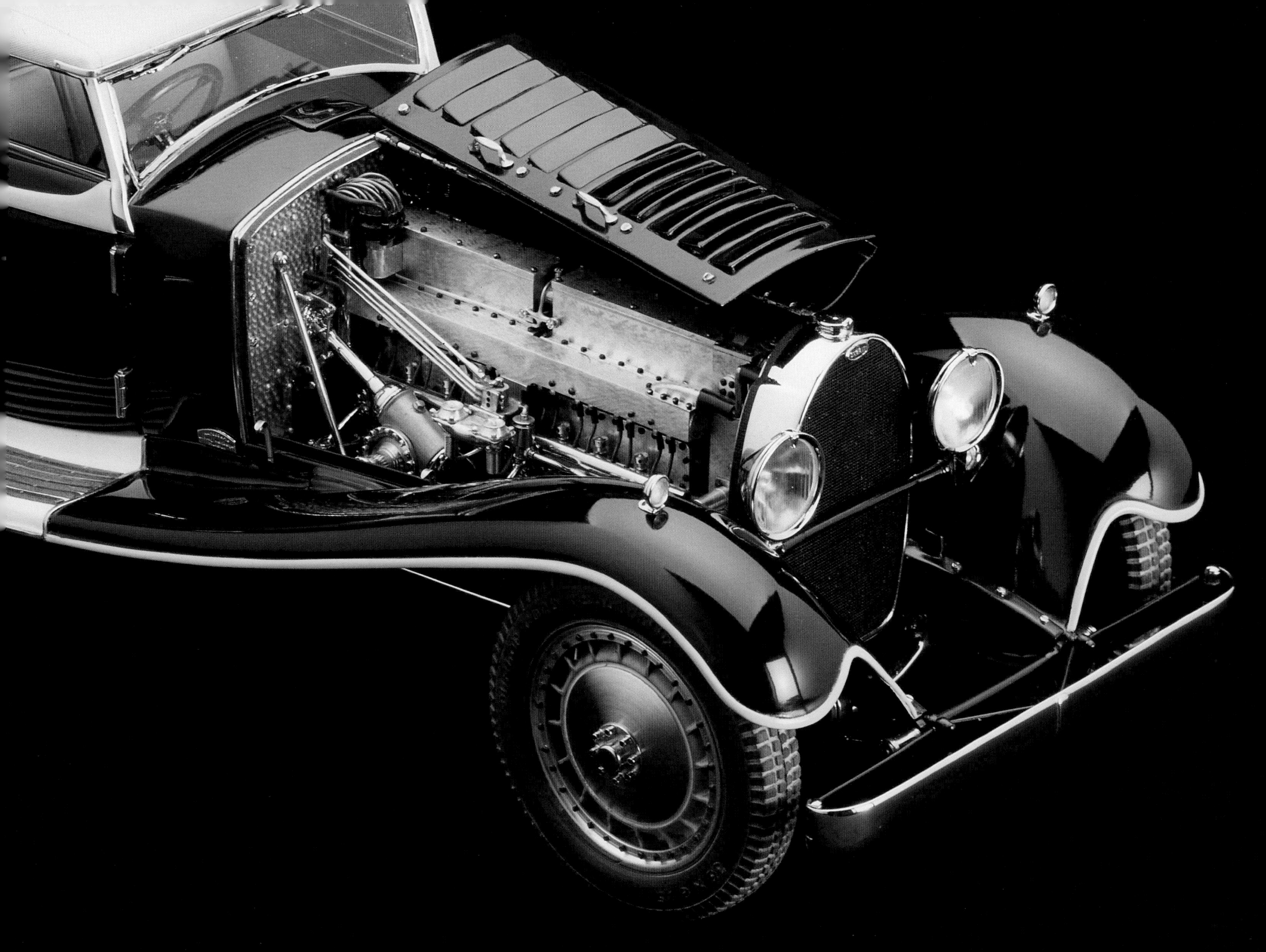

RIGHT: 1932 Bugatti Type 41 Royale (No. 41121) by Weinberger, as originally designed.

BELOW: Bugatti Type 41 Royale (No. 41121) by Weinberger, as rebuilt by Charles Chayne in 1947.

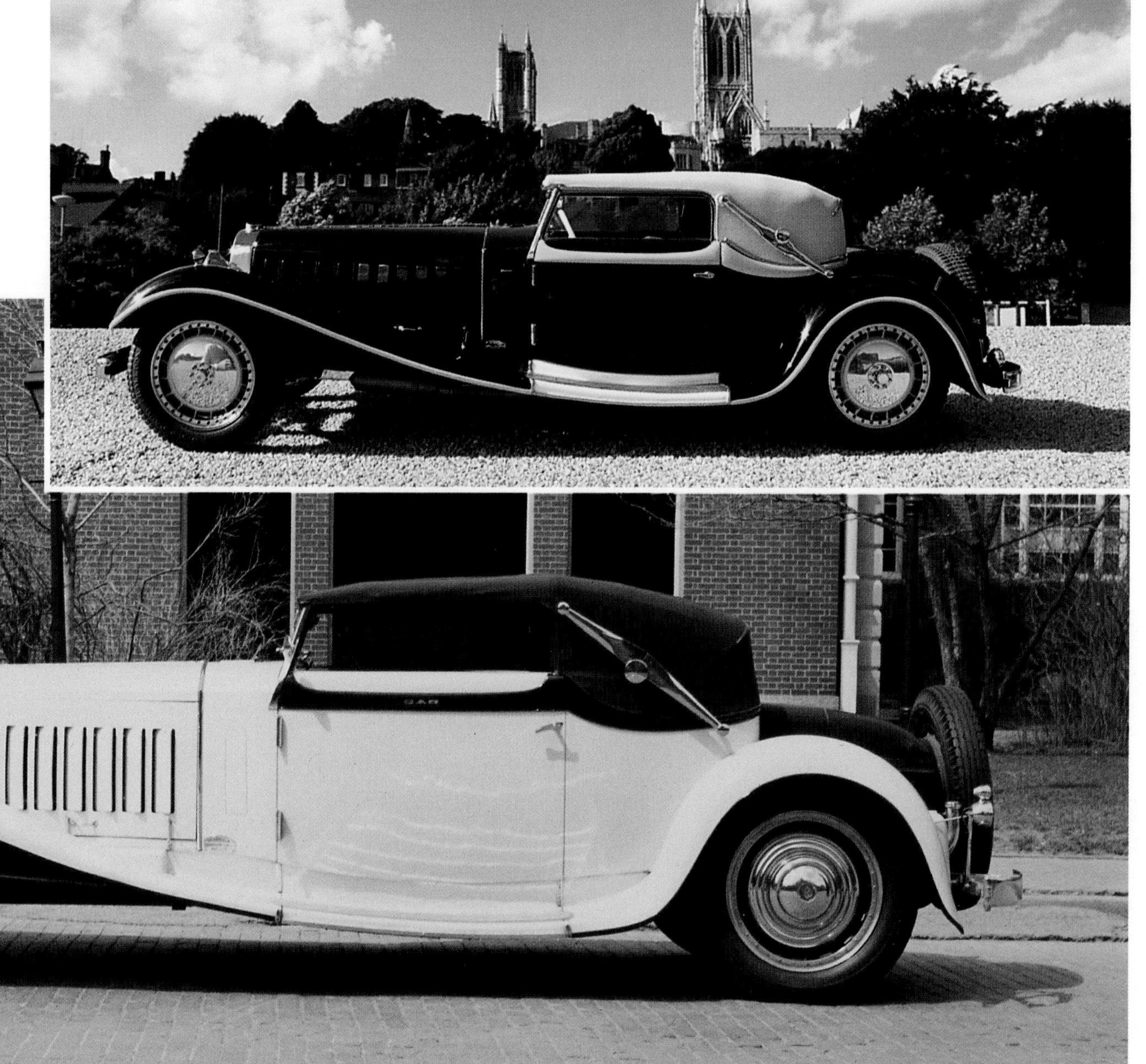

I was not long into the research for this car when I came upon the oft-told and printed tale, as follows: the Bugatti Royale was built for a Dr Josef Fuchs for the equivalent of $43,000 in 1932. In 1937 he took it to Shanghai and then to the USA, where, in the 1940s, it was rescued from a New York scrapyard by Charles Chayne, who restored it to its present state and presented it to the Henry Ford Museum. However, no one I contacted could shed any light on where this information had come from or add further details to authenticate and/or elaborate on it. Being of an age that recognizes some historical significance in these dates, and a sucker for research, it occurred to me that it could be fascinating, not only to find out what the Weinberger Royale originally looked like, but also to find out who Dr Fuchs was, and the significance of his travels three-quarters of the way around the globe with such an enormous car. In the course of the following twenty-odd years, I spoke or corresponded with everyone who had had any connection with or knowledge of the early history of both Dr Fuchs and/or the car. Gradually, a most fascinating story emerged. Incidentally, the price paid for the car was DM157,000 or £10,651 ($37,321), and this in 1932 when a Phantom II Continental Rolls-Royce with touring saloon bodywork was priced at £2,425, and a J Duesenberg with custom bodywork was $18,000. The Weinberger Royale was thus one of the most expensive cars ever made.

Dr Josef Fuchs (J.F.) was born on 16 October 1890 in Zellhausen, Hessen (not far from Frankfurt am Main), the son of the local baker and one of seven children. A school report at age fourteen indicated a good aptitude, with good ability in Biology, Greek, Latin and French, but moderate in German. His education culminated in a Medical Degree from Friedrich-Wilhelm's University in Bonn on 6 July 1911, and he stayed on to study for his Doctorate of medicine. In February 1914 he was called up for military service, shortly before his graduation from Bonn, which had to be delayed until after the war had ended. Part of his time in the army as a medical orderly was probably spent at the hospital in Pasewalk, where, in October 1918, Adolf Hitler was brought in with others suffering the effects of a gas attack. In fact, Dr Fuchs and Hitler, who was just one year older, appear to have been in the same place at the same time on a number of occasions. In 1920, J.F. moved to Munich after completing studies in gynaecology, where he rented an apartment in Thierschstrasse, and took up a post in a local hospital. Later, Hitler would also take an apartment in the same street, at No. 41. J.F. would have seen at first hand the degradation of the German people at the time of the Great Inflation – for example, in 1913 a dozen eggs cost less than one DM, but by 1923 just one egg was to cost eighty thousand million DM. Money had become worthless and barter was the order of the day. If one had gold, gems, foreign currency or works of art, it was possible to get by until they ran out. However, some people did become very rich at this time, and a doctor and gynaecologist offering essential services is likely to have been among these.

Not far from the end of Thierschstrasse was the Café Heck on the Galerienstrasse, Hitler's favourite watering hole, and a little further in town, the Hofbräuhaus where Hitler held his rowdy meetings. By the mid 1920s, J.F. had moved to Nuremberg, and after several changes of address, he settled into an apartment at Kopernicusplatz 24, just inside the city wall, with his own clinic and operating theatre at Koenig Str. 74. Nuremberg was the chosen venue for the Nazi Party rallies at the Zeppelinwiese, close by the city, the first being held there in August 1927 with an attendance of about 160,000. By 1933, the year that Dr Fuchs left, 250 trains were to bring in over 400,000 party members, and these rallies would take over the city for a week, with massive military parades.

By the early 1930s, J.F. had made a name for himself as a concert pianist, a surgeon, being the first in Germany to use spinal anaesthesia in assisting childbirth, a racing driver owning his own transporter and a pair of Bugatti Type 35s, and he was among the first to use a hard crash helmet in racing. He had a very plush apartment full of works of art, Persian rugs and a grand piano, and the apartment was often bedecked with flowers since he was very popular with the ladies. He appeared to know all the right people and was a friend of Ettore

LEFT AND BELOW LEFT: Two photographs from Ludwig Weinberger Jr, taken by Dr Fuchs the spring of 1932 when he collected the car from the Weinberger workshop in Munich, Germany.

BELOW: Ludwig Weinberger Jr at his 8m-long drawing board, on which he laid out the original design for the Bugatti Royale Cabriolet body in 1931.

Bugatti. All this was recalled by Horst Lattke, a young man in his late teens in the early 1930s who knew him very well, and who often accompanied J.F. and Lola Fine, J.F.'s office assistant, on picnics in the Bugatti Royale.

In 1929, J.F. exchanged the two Bugatti Type 35s for a Bugatti Type 46 and commissioned Carrossier Ludwig Weinberger of Munich to create the bodywork. The new body was to be the forerunner of that fitted three years later on the Type 41, except that the front wings stopped at the front door hinge and no running boards were fitted. In early 1931, J.F. placed the order for a Type 41 Bugatti chassis to be delivered to Carrossier Ludwig Weinberger in Munich for the fitting of a Cabriolet body. Josef Rietmaier was in charge of its building, which took three months and was under the supervision of an official from the Bugatti Works at Molsheim. On 25 March 1931, *Autocar* reported 'The first Golden Bug, the most expensive car in the world, is about to be delivered to M. Henri Esders in Paris. The second car is to the order of a famous German Surgeon.'

In October 1931, J.F. took delivery of a two-seater light aircraft (D-2170), a Klem L26AX. At about this time he was making a number of visits to Davos, internationally renowned as a health resort with several of the finest sanatoria in Switzerland, where he become a consultant. Among the personalities he met there was Madam Chiang Kai-Shek, wife of the Chinese Nationalist leader, Generalissimo Chiang Kai-Shek (an uncle of J.F.'s was the German Council General in Shanghai).

The consensus of opinion of those who lived through this period is that J.F. would have been becoming ever more aware of the growing political storm, and was probably making plans to remove himself and his money out of Germany, should the need arise. Being a Bugatti enthusiast, what more innocent way could there be but to invest a large part of his wealth in a Bugatti Royale. Although by name and countenance he might have appeared to the Nazis as being a Jew, he was in fact a Roman Catholic, having been educated at a Catholic school, then university, and at the end of his life, he donated money in his will to a Catholic church in New York.

On 30 January 1933, Adolf Hitler was appointed Reich Chancellor by Reich President von Hindenberg, and on 27 February the Reichstag parliament building was burnt down, which was interpreted by the Nazi leadership as the start of a communist uprising. The next day, the State suspended all civil rights, and mass arrests of communists and other left-wing opponents started to take place. J.F.'s two mechanics disappeared and he did not see them again. On 20 March, Heinrich Himmler, as chief of the SS, announced the establishment of the first concentration camp at Dachau. In May, J.F. was advised by a friend that he was on an SS list of Jews in the city. Arrangements were immediately put in hand to have the Bugatti Royale returned to Molsheim (in France) for servicing. Towards the end of June, Horst Lattke, who had been taking flying lessons with J.F. for the past two years, received a note to meet him at the airfield at Fürth, just outside Nuremberg. J.F. had been making arrangements to fly down to Italy to purchase a new Italian plane better suited for aerobatics. However, when Horst got to the airfield he found J.F. was already in the Klem, and after helping J.F. to strap himself in, Horst was shaken by the hand and told by J.F. that he would never see him again. Mystified, the young man returned to the city to find that Lola and the smaller Bugatti had gone and the apartment and the clinic were closed.

It transpired that from the beginning of July 1933, Dr Fuchs was to be forbidden to treat sick patients on account of his 'unworthy conduct', a Nazi phrase meaning 'exclusion from profession' by Government ruling for Jewish doctors in respect of treating anyone of Aryan race. In the meantime, J.F. had not flown to Italy, but to Zurich in Switzerland where he met up with Lola who had driven the Bugatti Type 46 there from Nuremberg. The two settled in Davos until early 1934, when they arranged passage to Shanghai. The Klem and smaller Bugatti were sold in Switzerland and M Band of Ateliers Bugatti in Paris arranged for the Bugatti Royale to be shipped to Shanghai from Trieste in Italy. It arrived there on 9 March 1934, J.F. and Lola having already arrived there on the seventh aboard the Italian Passenger Liner SS *Conte Russo*. They took up residence in the

ABOVE LEFT: Dr Josef Fuchs, a friend and Horst Lattke with the Klem D-2170.

ABOVE: The photo taken by Charles Chayne in 1937 showing the wood-rimmed steering wheel.

LEFT: Photo taken by Dr Fuchs of Horst and Lola with a pair of terriers given to him by Ettore Bugatti, out for a picnic with the big car.

Sassoon House (rooms 103 and 104), one of the most luxurious hotels in Shanghai, later to become famous as the Cathay Hotel. He also set up a private hospital at 811 Avenue Petain, still regarded as being the most elegant quarter in Shanghai, and became the personal physician to Madam Chiang Kai-Shek.

At this time, the Japanese army had taken over Manchuria on the northern borders of China and was about to move south, seeing that China was in a very weak state because of the civil war between Mao Tse-tung's Communist Party and the Nationalists under Generalissimo Chiang Kai-Shek. Being very aware of the fragile state of the country, J.F. soon applied to the American Consulate-General for a quota visa to enter the USA, but he kept being sidelined month after month without explanation. What J.F. did not know was that when a visa application arrived in Washington a check is made with the Bureau of Narcotics who maintain a list of smugglers. An agent in Istanbul had sent in a note that a 'Fuks', Nationality Unknown, 'had been persistently reported over several years as a smuggler of narcotics into Tientsin'. This note had been attached to Dr Fuchs' visa application, and for the next two years held it up, the apparent aim being to try to prove that he was the 'Fuks' in the report. Much correspondence was exchanged between the US Consulates in Shanghai, Berlin, Istanbul and Washington on J.F.'s background and movements. His position was not helped when Lola left for Mexico with Anton Wirthmüller, a convicted narcotics smuggler who had been seen with J.F. In November 1936, things came to a head when J.F. found out the reason for the delays. He obtained a note of good character from the Commissioner of the Shanghai Municipal Police, and after explaining that he had only carried out an appendicitis operation on Wirthmüller, he was finally given his visa on 8 February1937 for entry into the USA.

By this time, the Japanese had invaded China and were advancing south without much opposition, and things were getting desperate in Shanghai, with everyone trying to leave. J.F. secured two first-class berths for himself and another doctor. and, together with the Bugatti Royale, sailed from Shanghai aboard the SS *Empress of Russia* on 4 April, bound for Vancouver, Canada, just a few weeks before the Japanese were fighting in the streets of the city. The American Consulate-General immediately telegraphed a note to Washington DC of J.F.'s departure, stating that he would be arriving on 19 April and planned to enter the USA at Blaine (a small border town) the following day. The Customs post at Blaine was warned and ordered to make a special search of his belongings for hidden narcotics. J.F. had apparently been tipped off about the trap set for him at Blaine, and when the SS *Empress of Russia* docked at Victoria, BC, just short of Vancouver, he managed to have the Bugatti Royale offloaded and transferred to the much smaller steamship, SS *Princess Charlotte*, and he arrived at 9.45pm on 20 April at Seattle. Chief Inspector Ballinger (of the US Customs Service) reported that 'included in his baggage declaration was a large Bugatti automobile, of Italian make.'

Lola Fine in the Bugatti Type 46 with identical Weinberger bodywork.

The car was stored overnight in the Customs Baggage area and carefully examined by the searching squad on the morning of 21 April. Nothing of a prohibited nature was found, nor any indications that the Doctor may have been involved in narcotics trafficking. J.F. drove across the continent to New York, arriving on 4 May, and booked into the Leo House on 332 West 23rd Street. This was part of a Roman Catholic organization called the St Raphael Society, administered by the Sisters of St Agnes for visiting German Immigrants to New York. When I come across this information in 1989, I phoned Leo House in New York, and after a short check through the books they confirmed the date and time of J.F.'s arrival as 7pm., and his booking into rooms 605 and 613, with his companion, the other doctor who had travelled with him from Shanghai.

I discussed this drive across the USA with Roger Barlow, journalist and author, who had driven from coast to coast over 100 times, and he suggested that the most direct route would be Seattle, Spokane, Sioux City, Chicago, New York, at 2,925 miles (4,706km). This, divided by the twelve days and by eight hours (driving by day only), would give an average speed of about 30mph (48km/h). He thought that for a first-time driver in the USA, piloting a 20ft-long car on the road system of 1937 with the steering wheel on the right-hand side, this would probably have been quite good going. The next time I found mention of the car is at the practice day of the Vanderbilt Cup Race at Roosevelt Speedway, Long Island, NY, which would have been on 3 or 4 July 1937. As mentioned earlier, Mr Chayne had made a note of seeing the Bugatti there, and in fact took several photographs of the car, but there is no note as to whether he ever met Dr Fuchs. In discussing my research with Hugh Conway, considered by many as the 'Pope' of all things Bugatti, he suggested that I speak with Bunny Phillips in California, whom he thought had met J.F. with the Royale at one time. O.A. 'Bunny' Phillips was a well-known Bugatti enthusiast who had a Bugatti Service Centre at 1222 North Western Avenue, Los Angeles, in 1937. My phone call to him was in June 1988, fifty years on. He answered the phone and when I explained my interest in J.F. and the Bugatti Royale, I just could not stop him – it was as if it had all happened yesterday.

Dr Fuchs had just driven down from Seattle and the engine was giving him a problem because 'the Champion R1S plugs that had been fitted were very cold racing plugs and prone to oiling up.' Bunny continued, 'So I fitted Champion C7s, which are hot and were used in the Ford V8s at the time. I also checked out the ignition system and adjusted the clutch. We drove out to Santa Monica for about an hour and he was very satisfied with what I had done and was confident he could now make it back to New York.' He also recalled that J.F. had stayed five days in L.A. at the Ambassador's Hotel, about 6 miles from Bunny's workshop. His only problem was that he could not put a date to all this, other than it was either 1937 or '38; however, he did recall that, 'I had just gotten out of hospital due to an accident at the Indianapolis 500.' Griff Borgeson, whose knowledge was legendary on such automotive matters, soon added the date. The accident happened when a crankshaft broke in a Duesenberg being driven by Bunny Phillips in late May 1937, so it would have been several months after this that he was able to work on J.F.'s car. This would indicate that J.F. had made at least three coast-to-coast crossings of the USA with the Weinberger Royale in 1937. In his renewed request for an immigrant visa back in February, it was listed that 'he had liquid assets of $18,736 and personal property of substantial value'. He probably would have returned to organize the transport of this to New York. Family members recall a grand piano among many other things that, it was said, had been shipped from Germany to China and then on to his apartment in New York.

As soon as he arrived in New York, he started to send letters and telegrams to his old university in Bonn for proof of his medical degree, without which he could not practise medicine. Obtaining these became quite desperate and it was not until 28 October that he received his licence. He set himself up with an office and an apartment at 87–59 171 Street Jamaica, in the Queens district of New York. Up to this point, Dr Fuchs seems to have led a charmed life, knowing all the right people, and just what to do at the right time to remove himself and the car out of harm's way just in the nick of time. Whether it was the stress of getting his licence to practise medicine, and setting up a new home and office, or just the relief of having arrived in a free country where he could at last settle down, it would appear that he just did not know what to expect from a New York winter. The big Bugatti was parked down the side of his apartment in Queens, with no protection from the weather. The radiator had most probably been flushed and refilled in California, and the 15 gallons of water in the radiator and engine froze, severely cracking the main engine block. With no way of getting this repaired or replaced (even General Motors did not make an engine this big), the Bugatti Royale was a complete write-off and so was J.F.'s investment, just when he needed it most.

A niece remembers visiting him as a child on a number of occasions shortly after this, and 'being in awe of his wonderful home. In the entrance hall was displayed a huge Buddha. There were oriental rugs throughout the home and he also had a grand piano which he played for us each time we came to visit. He was a very generous man and offered to put my father through medical school, if he so desired.' By the 1950s he had moved to Merrick Road, Lynbrook, Nassau County, NY, where he died on 17 August 1968 (just two months before I started my career in model engineering). He is buried in Cressona, PA.

But what of the car? It remained under a canvas cover alongside J.F.'s apartment for three years. David Uihlein recalled going to see it as a twenty-year old in 1940. Being crazy about Bugattis, especially about owning a Type 35 (a very small racing model), he had been given a lead on the Bugatti from a dealer on Broadway. 'I scurried out to Long Island, pressed Dr Fuchs's doorbell and he graciously permitted me to go in his backyard where the Bugatti was under canvas. I was astounded and amazed, as I had never heard or seen such a huge Bugatti. I remember raising the canvas and looking at the gigantic radiator and saying to myself, "My God, it's too big".' Within a week he had told John Oliveau, a partner with George Rand, who had an office and workshop trading and servicing exotic cars at a large warehouse complex close to the end of the 59th Bridge, on the East River called 'The Brewster Building'. In a very short time, they had the Bugatti in the workshop, 'but the Doctor didn't want to spend a nickel on repairs.' The car stayed there for a couple of years until the army requisitioned the building for war work, when the car was towed back to Dr Fuchs.

The Brewster Building was a mecca for car enthusiasts, and we spoke with a number of people who saw the Bugatti there and were offered it at ever lower prices. Henry Austin Clark Jr, famous for his Automobile Collection and library, remembered being offered it for $1,250, while Richard H. Rush in his book, *Automobiles as Investment*, recalled being offered the car for $600. Bunny Phillips was visiting The Brewster Building in 1941 and would have been interested, except that he already had a race car on a trailer in tow that he was taking back to Los Angeles. The price to him was $450. Roger Barlow appears to have been one of the last to see the car in The Brewster Building, when he called by to see John Oliveau in late 1942, when he and his business was about to be evicted to make room for war work. He was storing about ten cars, all of which had to go, and his biggest problem was the Bugatti Royale, 'sitting in a dusty corner looking the worse for wear.'

'Pay the storage, it's about $350, and take it away so my biggest worry will be over,' he was told, 'Only you cannot drive it as the block is cracked.' He did not buy the car as he had other things on his mind, not least being on honeymoon and having just been inducted into the Navy. The Japanese had attacked Pearl Harbor on 7 December 1941, and collecting old cars was at the bottom of most people's lists of things to do – except for one person, Charles Chayne. After the car was returned to J.F., the Doctor stored it for a short while until he moved to smaller accommodation at 45 E. 9th Street, whereupon he sent the Bugatti to a wreckers' yard in the Bronx, Sam's Junk Yard, on Randall Avenue. Dale McCauley had just joined the OCS Signal Core at Fort Monmouth, New Jersey, and as part

THIS PAGE:
LEFT: Saved from the crushers, in Mr Chayne's driveway in Flint.
BELOW LEFT: Mr Chayne surveys the ravages of being left in the open through seven New York winters. Note the water staining of the Hungarian pigskin interior.
BELOW RIGHT: The main engine casting showing the two large cracks caused by water freezing in the engine in the winter of 1937.

OPPOSITE PAGE:
The big car in storage at the Brewster Building before going to Sam's Junk Yard.

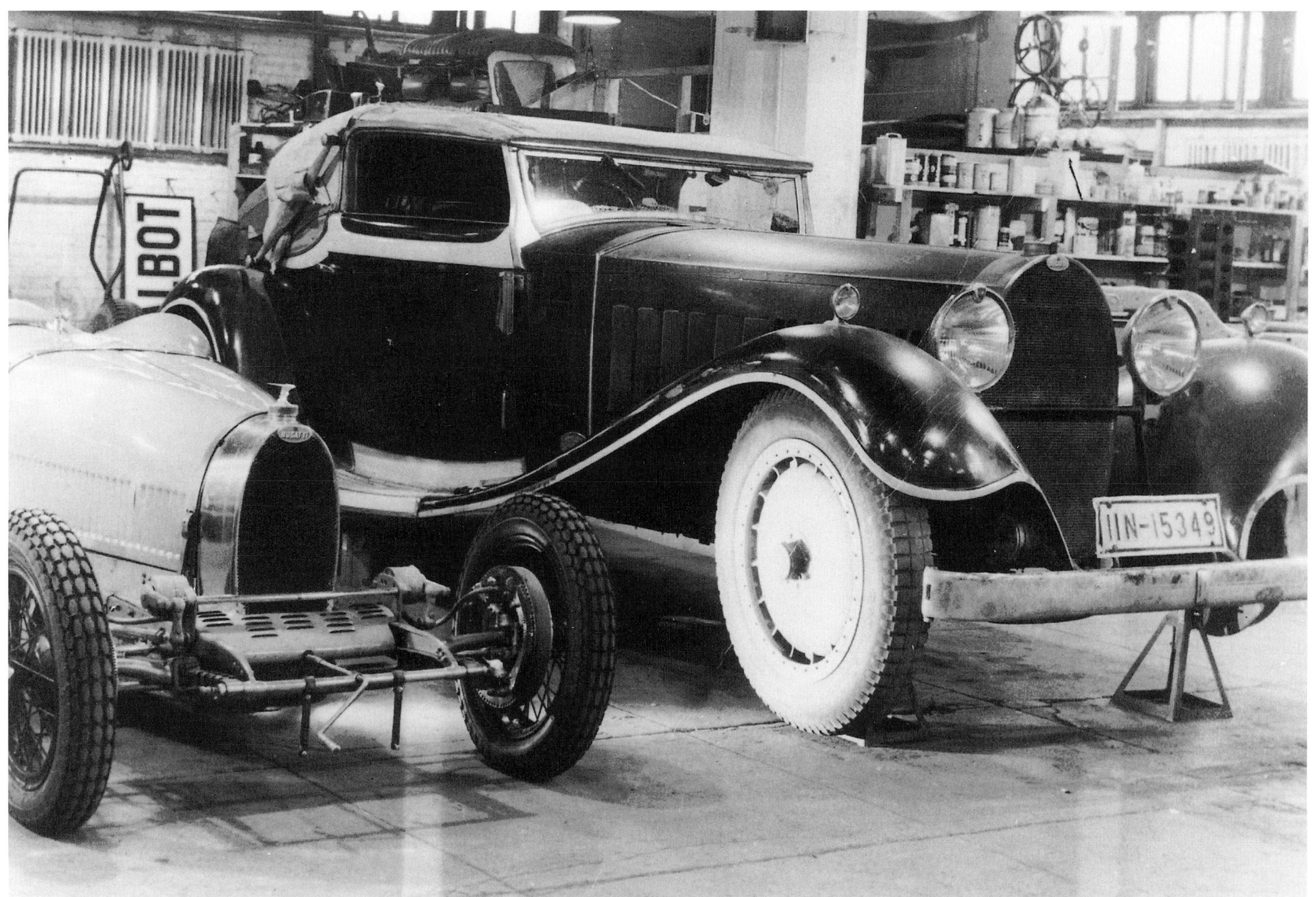
IIN-15349

of the training they were given copies of *The Wall Street Journal* to read, 'to sophisticate the farm boys,' as he put it. In the auto section of his edition was an advertisement for a Bugatti Royale, price $850, with a phone number. He called the number to get the address and the following Sunday went out to the scrapyard, and there through the fence was the Weinberger Bugatti Royale, standing with a number of other junked cars near a small brick building. Dale told us that he had $924 in the bank, and had it been a Duesenberg he would have bought it. So yet another missed the chance of a lifetime.

LEFT: Charles Chayne in 1947 with his rebuilt Weinberger Bugatti Royale. Note the chrome crossbar and additional driving lights and air horns, all obscuring that beautiful Bugatti radiator.

Mr and Mrs Charles A. Chayne in September 1959 presenting the big car to the Henry Ford and Greenfield Village Museum.

Charles Chayne received a phone call from a friend in early June 1943 that the Bugatti Royale had been seen in Sam's Junk Yard. He phoned Charles Stitch, who managed a foreign car shop in New York, to purchase the car on his behalf and store it for him until he could have it moved back to his home in Flint, Michigan. Dale McCauley told us that he saw the car again sometime in 1946, when he was asked by a friend to call by his garage for his opinion about a cracked engine block, as he made a speciality of repairing them. The garage was on the corner of John R. and 7 Mile (roads) in Detroit. When he arrived there it was on a Haul-Away transporter, with three other vehicles, presumably bound for Flint for a rebuild. In early 1947 the car was reborn, though very considerably changed, and driven on the Glidden Tour of the Veteran Motor Car Club of America. It was regularly seen on such outings for the next several years, until in September 1959, when Mr & Mrs Chayne officially presented it to the Henry Ford Museum, where it has been on public display ever since.

In 1990, we had the very good fortune to be invited to a reunion of all six of the original Bugatti Royales at the Musée National de l'Automobile 'Collection Schlumpf' at Mulhouse in Alsace, France. It was a very memorable occasion, not least for us, seeing again the Weinberger Bugatti Royale, which, having been flown in from the Ford Museum in the USA, had now completed a circumnavigation of the globe, its birthplace being at Molsheim just 50 miles up the road.

So how much is the car worth now, that Roger Barlow had turned down for just $350? A recent sale of one of its sisters would indicate perhaps in the region of ten million dollars.

This is only a brief summary of the information that has been collected, and it is still coming in. However, one cannot amass data to this extent without the help and cooperation of others. It has been a curious fact that no member of the Fuchs family, including his niece, knew anything of his ownership of this car. A number of enthusiasts had snippets of information, some fact, some fiction, that seemed to fire their imagination and so greatly assisted my endeavours. I would like to thank in particular Randy Mason for opening the archives of the Henry Ford Museum totally for my research, and for passing all leads regarding the Weinberger Bugatti Royale to me for further investigation. Also Dr Hannelore Theodor, Der Generalkonsul Der Bundesrepublik Deutschland in Shanghai, Erik Eckermann in Germany and Horst Lattke and Norey Fuchs-Gallo for so freely recounting their personal memories of Dr Josef Fuchs.

Horst Lattke and Randy Mason at the grave of Dr Josef Fuchs in 1987.

Bugatti Type 57sc Atlantic and Corsica

OPPOSITE: 1938 Bugatti Type 57sc Atlantic with full engine and chassis detail in one-fifteenth scale.

WHEN I FIRST SAW THIS CAR, I VIEWED IT WITH THE PECULIAR FASCINATION that one feels when meeting the sort of woman who, though not beautiful, exudes class and personality from her very fingertips. They both have voluptuous curves and from some angles are perfection, but from others the proportions and lines can seem just a little too way-out for my particular taste. However, a closer look will reveal that we are in the presence of someone with a pedigree of distinction.

The line from which the car descends started in 1935 when the first Type 57S was completed. Although the body was that of an open two-seater Torpedo, it did feature the riveted ribs over the wings and bodywork that is so much a feature of this car. The second car, a coupé, was built looking very much like our subject – the main difference being a flat radiator and moulded-in headlamps – and was built for exhibition, although it was also used by Ettore Bugatti as his own private car. In early 1936, a third T57S appeared with a coupé body and redesigned radiator, which was now set lower and of 'V' shape. The headlights appear in early photographs to have been set into the fairings inboard of the wings in a similar way to our car, though much lower down. However, in 1939 this car was rebodied and fitted with a supercharger. This Aerolith now resides in the USA and has faired-in headlights featuring a riveted rib back from the top centre of each lamp to match the body and wings.

In December 1936, a new T57S coupé appeared with almost identical bodywork, and with the new designation 'Atlantic'. This car also underwent surgery, some of which was disastrous in the extreme. In 1939, the rear wings were reshaped from the characteristic wrap-around of the original design to a straight ribbed pontoon to match those at the front. The headlights were raised and faired-in, fog lamps fitted underneath, and a louvred bonnet replaced the wire mesh-sided original. The colour was also changed from black to blue. In 1955, the car came into conflict with a railcar and was cut in two. Now, after many years of painstaking work, it has been rebuilt to its original specifications and colour scheme.

Our model is patterned after what is probably the most original of these cars. It was delivered in May 1938 to someone of tall stature, as the roof line is slightly higher on this than on the other cars. I was also told by someone familiar with the history of the car that the blue is original and was chosen to match the then owner's fiancée's sapphire ring, a nice story but I have not as yet been able to corroborate it. In the late 1970s, when I met the car for the first time and collected the data for the plans, the car was believed not to have gone through the drastic facelifting exercises of its other family members. As far as I was aware, the only major deviation from 'as built' were the headlights, which, on the car then, did not fit the moulded shape provided for them in the front wings. It is thought that the originals were stolen some years ago, but this has been corrected on all of the miniatures.

1938 Bugatti Atlantic in the Lincolnshire countryside.

Sadly, in the late 1990s this very original masterpiece was subjected to the whims of a new owner, and, in a total rebuild, emerged painted black, with disc wheels and skirts to the rear wings among other things. Like the Weinberger Bugatti Royale, the basic car is still with us, and, who knows, maybe one day both cars will be restored back to their former glory. However much we may bristle, and very many enthusiasts for originality do, at the indignities perpetrated on these historic relics (it is like painting the hair of the Mona Lisa blonde because that is your preference), we do have to thank the owners for saving and maintaining these cars for posterity.

Eleven miniatures of the 1938 Bugatti Atlantic have been built, nine with full engine and chassis detail and two without, as curbside examples. All have been built to a scale of one to fifteen. I so enjoyed building the type 57sc engine and chassis, that I started to look around for a body style more to my own personal liking, and came upon a book illustration showing one fitted with an English body by Corsica of London. I asked around those in the know on most things Bugatti and classic cars in general, but no one could come up with the current owner, or of the car's whereabouts. It apparently had not been seen for some considerable time, nor written up in the motoring press for many years. Then about six months later, a large stiff brown envelope arrived in the post and inside were two ten by eight colour photographs of the 1938 Bugatti Type 57sc with Corsica body, with a request to have a miniature made of it. Who says there is no such thing as telepathy?

The owner of the car had sent the photographs, along with a request that the next time we were in his area we were invited to collect the necessary dimensions and photographs for the plans. This was another very original car, with only minor changes, apart from the seats and dashboard, which had both been refurbished. This was most probably because both had originally been upholstered in crocodile leather, which may well not have been an ideal choice for an open sports car subjected to the vagaries of an English climate. Five of these miniatures have been built with full engine and chassis detail to one-fifteenth scale, all with simulated crocodile leather dashboards and seats. Phyllis reproduced each of the 'scales' forming the patterns exactly to scale from an original piece of full-size crocodile leather. I'm pleased to say that the owner has now restored the original interior with crocodile leather to match his miniature.

OPPOSITE: 1938 Bugatti Type 57sc Atlantic engine detail in one-fifteenth scale.

The Bugatti Owners Club journal, *Bugantics*, of September 1938 carries a very nice article of the period that illustrates perfectly the feelings that can be engendered by some cars. The article is by Colonel G.B.Giles, founder member of the club and original owner of this car. Col Giles owned several Bugatti cars, to which he gave names – there was 'Flora' and 'Thérése' and la petite 'Sezanne', the last being the Corsica Type 57sc. On seeing the newly arrived chassis from Molsheim, with Eric the body designer, he wrote, 'What a thrill! Eric and I dashed down and saw this marvellous chassis in all its nakedness, and really it is very marvellous, the tremendous strength of the chassis, the beautifully finished engine, the built-in De Rams, the tremendous brakes with their tapered finely

Bugatti Type 57sc Atlantic showing the interior.

ribbed drums and the hundreds of other interesting points. After spending about an hour we tore ourselves away, and the following day she went to Corsica.'

Of the car's performance, Giles wrote, 'The safe maximum revs are 5,500, giving approximately 60 [mph] in bottom, 80 in second, 100 in third and 120 in top, and this can be achieved at any time the driver feels inclined. Yet in London, the car can be driven at 10mph without snatch and with a clean pick-up, and this with a compression of over 10 to 1, a truly remarkable car.' And on parking: 'The whole result, I am afraid, is so striking that whenever the car is left a very large crowd gathers around, which is, at times, somewhat embarrassing, as at one motor race meeting the crowd grew to such dimensions that when I wanted to go home I was accused of trying to work my way to the front of the crowd. But on timidly explaining that I would be so grateful if I might take my car away, I was allowed to sit in it and start the engine.'

OPPOSITE: 1938 Bugatti Type 57sc, with body by Corsica, with full engine and chassis detail in one-fifteenth scale.

The Corsica Bugatti Type 57sc at home.

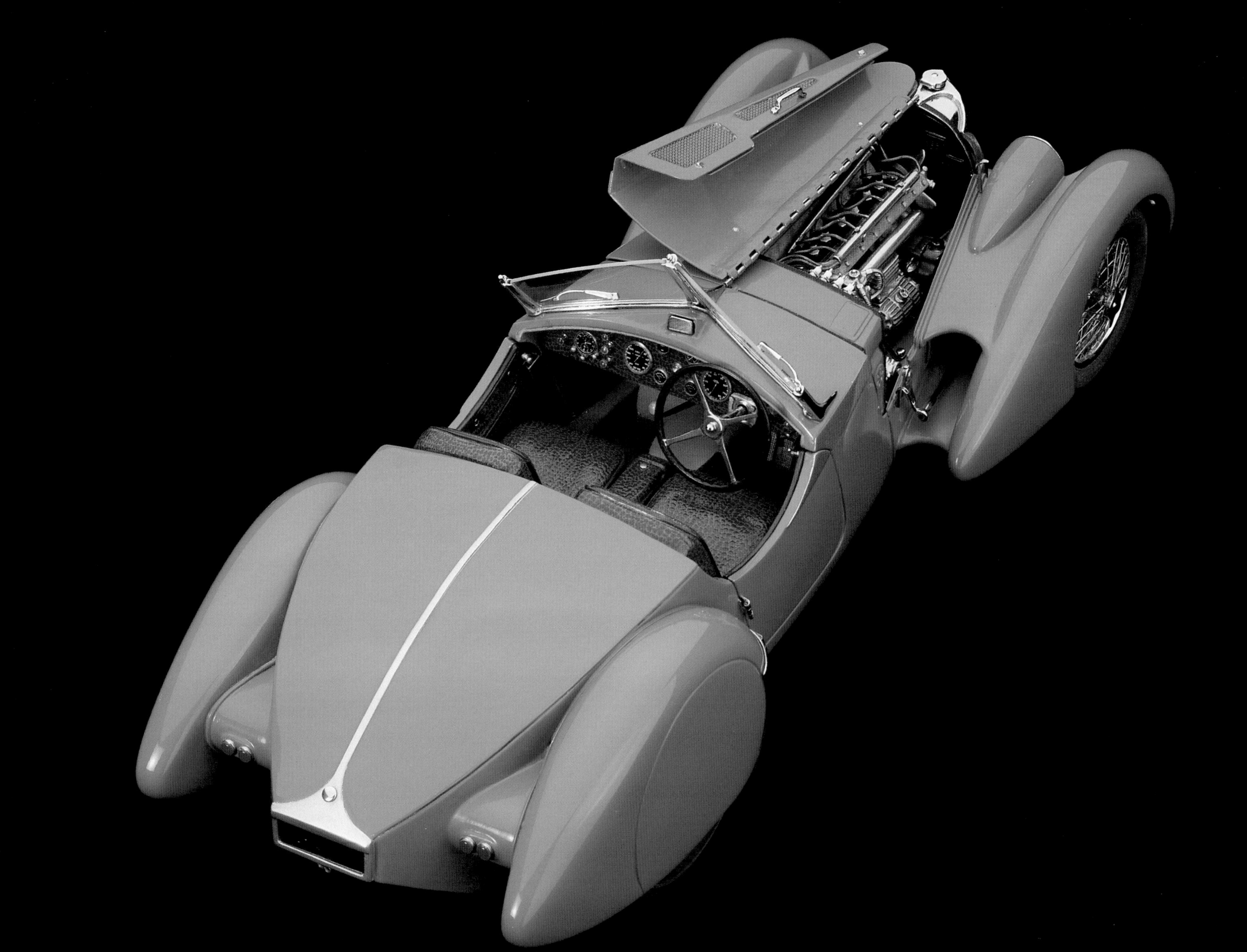

Bugatti Type 59

OPPOSITE: 1932 Bugatti Type 59, built with full engine and chassis detail in one-fifteenth scale.

MY FEELINGS HAVE ALWAYS BEEN THAT WHEELS ARE TO A CAR AS LEGS ARE to a woman; if they are attractive and the bodywork is of classic proportions, the whole is a beauty to behold. What better example of this could one have than the Type 59 Bugatti? Those wheels from the hand of Ettore Bugatti, extremely expensive to make and not the most practical in use, are undoubtedly, for me at least, the most beautiful wire wheels that ever graced a car. For Bugatti, the Type 59 was almost the end of a line in Grand Prix cars. It arrived on the scene just when the German 'Auto Union' and 'Mercedes-Benz' cars were about to make their mark. The Type 59 was of traditional Bugatti styling that went back to the 1920s, whereas its up and coming rivals were about to set new standards of streamlining that would stay with us well after the 1939–45 war. It was not so much this that prevented the new Bugatti from re-establishing itself at the forefront of motor racing, but more the almost unlimited political funds that went towards making the German cars reign supreme.

The wheels are unconventional in the extreme, in that the spokes not only radiate out from the centre in straight lines but also absorb only the radial loads on the wheel. The power and braking loads are taken by numerous teeth cut on flanges cast on the two sections of the wheel and brake drum. The actual wheels are made from two aluminium castings. The rim has a set of gear-cut teeth located around a flange on the inside at the back. The brake drum and the hub together form the second casting with a set of gear-cut teeth to match, cut around a flange on the brake drum. When assembled with the spokes, the two sets of teeth perfectly mesh together.

Because of the limitations of aluminium, the wheels made for the miniatures have been machined from brass stock, then polished and chrome-plated before spoking. Each wheel was made in two parts, after which it was provided with the requisite number of spoke holes. The two parts were first located so that the spoke holes lined up perfectly, then forced together as a press fit. This had the advantage that no spoking jig was necessary for assembling the spokes. That was the plus side. The downside was that great care was needed to drill the front row of spoke holes on the wheel hub. Thirty-two holes, each of just twelve-thousandths of an inch in diameter, were required to be drilled on a circumference that spaced them just twenty-two thousandths of an inch apart. This meant that there was less metal left between the holes than the holes were in diameter. Using special Swiss-made drills and a steady hand, each wheel was provided with 160 spoke holes, that is, 640 per set, per car. The remainder of the building followed my usual practice of working from the ground up. In all, nine miniatures have been built with full engine and chassis detail.

Type 59 Bugatti in the Lincolnshire countryside.

Cord 812 Models

OPPOSITE: 1938 Cord 812 Coupé showing engine detail built to a scale of one-fifteenth.

THE CORD 812 IS ALSO 'AUTOMOTIVE ART' PERFECTED. IT IS NOT ONLY beautiful (and not a personal design created for a single client as was the Weinberger Bugatti Royale), but was designed and built as a production car to appeal to the general public – and they loved it. It was and still is a design of car that a lot of people aspire to own, not for an incredible performance or drivability, which are both acceptable, but because of its presence – it is Rolling Sculpture, to quote the title of a book on the work of Gordon M. Buehrig, its designer. The car was first shown to the public at the Automobile Manufacturers Association show in New York in December 1935 and it created a sensation. The small group of six cars on the Cord stand were standing on the floor rather then on pedestals, which made it difficult for the crowds of people thronging around to see them. Other manufacturers on nearby stands complained bitterly about people clambering on to their cars to get a better view of those on the Cord stand. Press and public comments were rapturous, and orders flooded in, which was unfortunate because the manufacturing problems for such a revolutionary car had not yet been sorted out, and many of the customers who were expecting to take delivery of a new car early in the new year received in place of it a one thirty-second scale miniature in bronze, compliments of the 'Cord Corporation'.

I will have more to say with regard to Gordon M. Buehrig when we discuss the Duesenbergs, but suffice to say here that for a lifetime's work in the automotive industry and principally for his design of the Cord 810/812 series, and his work at Duesenberg, he was selected by the Society of Automotive Historians as one of the industry's thirty most significant people internationally. In October 1989, he was inducted into the Automotive Hall of Fame, the single greatest honour for anyone who has dedicated their life to the automotive industry. In 1951 the New York Museum of Modern Art created a special exhibit comprising eight cars that they considered to be the finest automotive designs of all time, and an Cord 812 was one of them. The Curator of Architecture at the Museum writing to Gordon on the reason behind the choice of the Cord, said '... the originality of the conception and the skill with which its several parts have been realized makes it one of the most powerful designs in the exhibition ...'.

The Cord 810 was the first production car to have front-wheel drive and a monocoque construction. Up to this time, the standard layout was for a ladder-type chassis frame to provide the main strength of the vehicle, with the body bolted on for the accommodation, engine at the front and drive wheels at the rear. By doing away with the chassis frame and designing the additional strength into the bodywork and then putting the driving wheels at the front with the engine, it made for a much lower style, lighter and more stable car. Also, with no driveshaft going to the rear wheels, the floorpan could be made flat, making more interior space available. Among the many innovations were the concealed headlights that fold out for night-time use, and fold away flush with the front wings when not

Cord 812 Coupé photographed in Lincolnshire.

ABOVE: The first two Cord chassis under construction.

RIGHT: Fully detailed Cord 812 chassis, together with a Cord Coupé, showing the opened rumble seat.

ABOVE: Body pattern and chassis, with the start of the body panels.

ABOVE RIGHT: Body patterns, together with the assembly of the first body parts.

OPPOSITE: 1938 Cord 812 rolling chassis built to a scale of one-fifteenth.

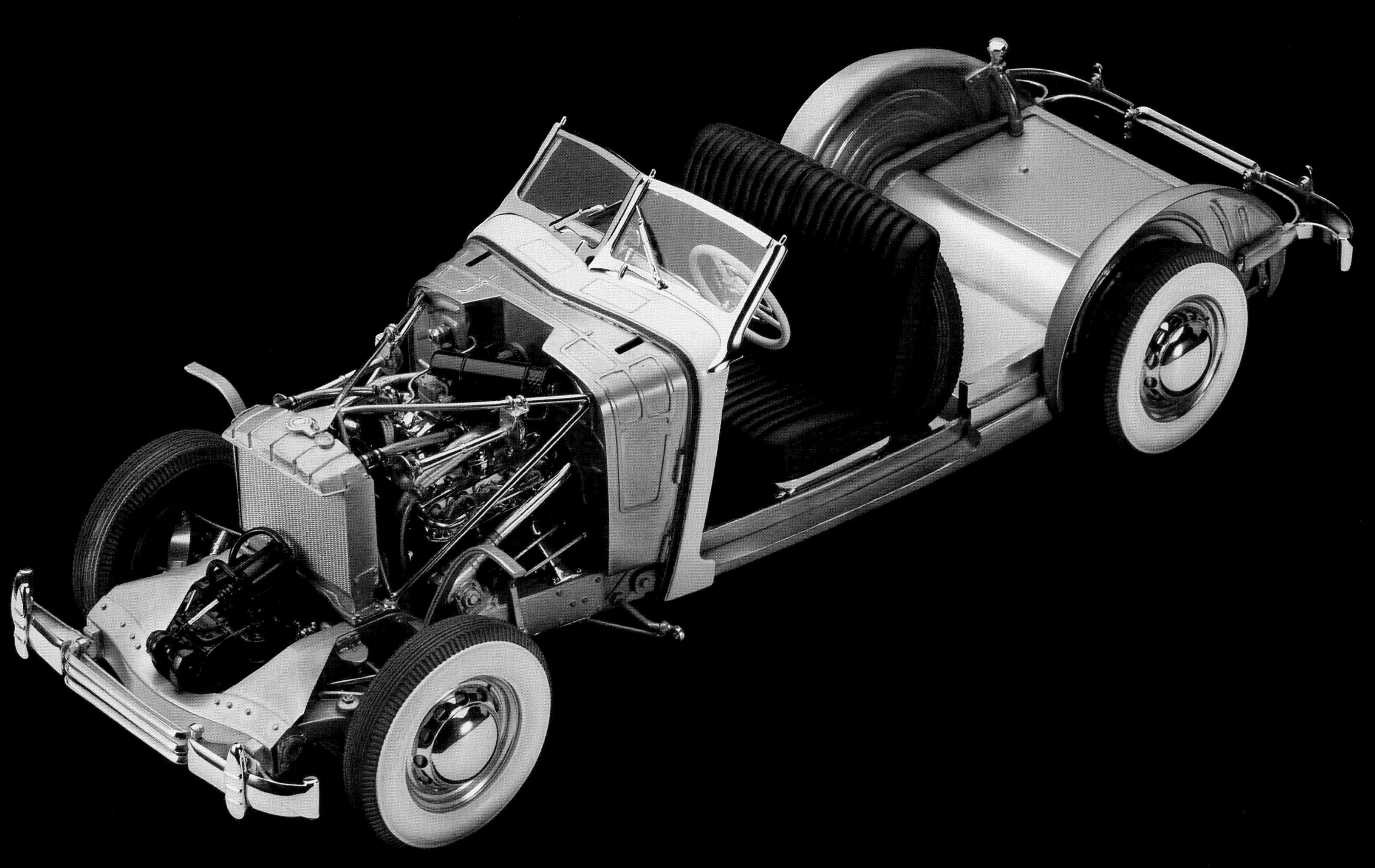

LEFT: 812 supercharged Cord miniature, complete and ready for painting and plating.

OPPOSITE: 1938 812 supercharged Cord, built with full engine and chassis detail in one-fifteenth scale.

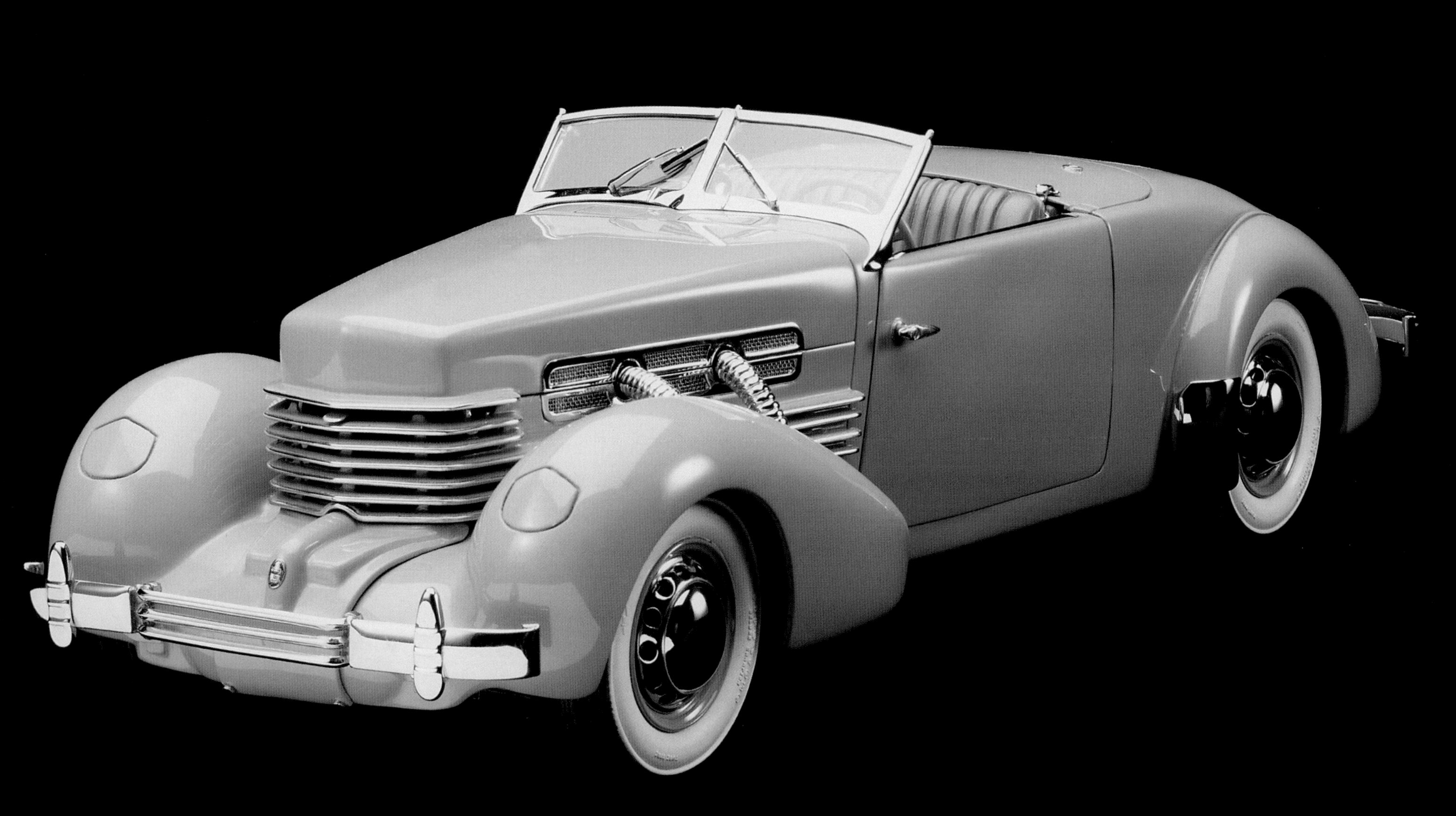

required. All of these and more we take for granted today, but in 1935 they were a revolution in design and saw the light of day for the first time on the Cord 810.

As may be imagined, recreating this in miniature was a very interesting exercise, not least where to start. The wheels presented few problems, but where was I going to put them without the usual 'I' beam front axle and half-elliptical spring suspension? Although there is a solid axle at the rear, suspended on half-elliptical springs in the conventional manner, there is no standard chassis to hang them on, and no front axle at all, just two radial girders that form the main elements of the independent front suspension. There is a short section of box girder at the front to carry the suspension, the V8 engine and gearbox, but it is exceedingly complex. Phyllis had produced the usual very accurate and highly detailed plans on the computer for the Cord, and by setting the various components on different layers in the CAD system we were able to map out accurately just where each of the components started from and went to. We were also able to extract three-view drawings for each of the components, in a way that would have been all but impossible were the plans hand-drawn to scale. One of the many advantages of the CAD system is that the plans are drafted at full size, and only printed at the final stage to a scale of one-fifteenth, so one can zoom in (to enlarge) an individual part. By following the computer drawings precisely, we were able to fabricate each of the parts from sheet brass, much as the originals had been fabricated from sheet steel, and assemble them to form the complex front unit of the box frame, suspension and engine mounts. The remainder of the lower body and floorpan were then fabricated from sheet brass and square tube to form a platform on which to hang all four wheels. I cannot express my admiration for the people who had to undertake this work in full size for the first time and make it work, on a tight budget of time and money, and by hand without the help of a computer. Ours is but a simple task in comparison.

As members of the Auburn Cord Duesenberg Club for a number of years and having attended many of their meetings, one has the chance to see cars in all stages of reconstruction. Members are always encouraged to bring along these part-built cars so that others can see and learn something of the problems encountered. For us, great advantage was taken in photographing every aspect of them, particularly those with the front wings and bonnet removed to show the mechanics. We also visited several cars under restoration to collect more data on component parts, as you really cannot see much that is recognizable under the bonnet of a Cord, except for a mass of pipes looking for all the world like a plumber's nightmare. When the commission finally arrived to produce a miniature, the background for the work was in place and the commission was eagerly accepted. The particular car for the first miniature was a rare 1938 Cord 812 Coupé with a rumble seat in place of the normal boot. Just four of these had been made by the factory. As Phyllis was completing the plans for this we received an enquiry for a second miniature, also a 1938 Cord 812 Coupé, but with supercharged engine and standard rear-end boot lid. So far, three miniatures have been built with full engine and chassis detail to a scale of one to fifteen, including one finished as a chassis.

OPPOSITE: Rear view of supercharged Cord, built with full engine and chassis detail in one-fifteenth scale.

Cord 812 Coupé photographed in Lincolnshire.

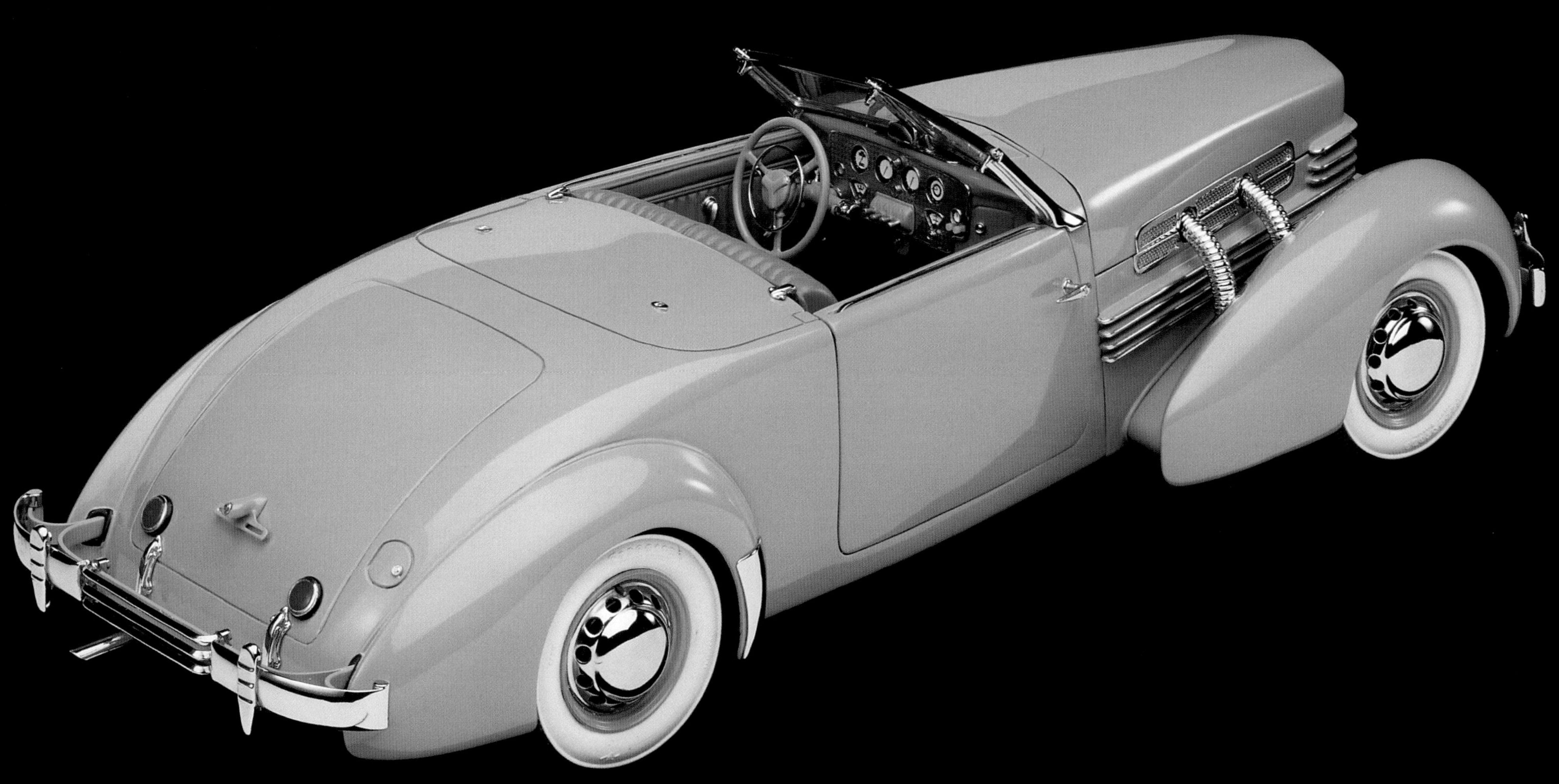

Duesenberg

OPPOSITE: 1929 'J' Duesenberg chassis, unpainted with full engine and chassis detail in one-fifteenth scale.

I CAME FACE TO FACE WITH MY FIRST DUESENBERG ON A VISIT TO THE Briggs Cunningham Collection, south of Los Angeles, in 1973. Or, rather, a pair of Duesenbergs, as Briggs had a Sweep Panel Dual Cowl Phaeton 'J' Duesey and the ex-Gary Cooper 'SSJ' Roadster 'J-563', which we later created in miniature for him. Briggs, like almost everyone we have met associated with these cars, was the most generous of people, and gave us open house with regard to the collection whenever we were in town. On many occasions, word would go out that the Wingroves were about and all manner of fascinating people from the classic car world would come down to visit. Twice, model shows and exhibitions were arranged in time for our visits. Briggs' Museum was a mecca for all those interested in the finer things of the automotive world, and, like the Harrah's Collection in Reno, is much missed now that it is no more. Of just over 360 'J' and 'SJ' cars built, it has been estimated from old factory records that there were just five chassis assembled with right-hand-drive steering. Of these, there has never been more than one at any single time in the UK over the past fifty years. The current example is 'J-489', a two-tone blue Derham Tourster, now resident at the Haynes Motor Museum in Sparkford, Somerset, so a visit to the USA is a must if you wish to see a selection these cars in the flesh.

My first encounter with Doc Elsner's Duesey at his home in Crete, Nebraska.

This first visit to California was a short one, and we stopped off at Crete, Nebraska, on our way home to have a more intimate look at 'the mightiest American automobile,' as it has been called, and with good reason. We had been invited to stay with Dr 'Doc' Carl Elsner, a very well-known character from the Duesenberg world of the 1970s and 80s. After joining the Auburn-Cord-Duesenberg Club, I started to correspond with several enthusiasts who owned or had knowledge of these cars. Such is the infectious enthusiasm generated around these cars, that in many cases we became long-standing friends and often exchanged visits, even thirty years on. Another friend from this early period is Robert 'Bob' Fabris, much-respected historian for most things connected with Duesenberg and Cord, and to whom we are greatly indebted for my particular education on these matters.

Doc Elsner was the very proud owner of a two-tone green Derham Tourster Duel Cowl Phaeton Duesenberg 'J-504'. The colours themselves are most uninspiring; the dark green is almost an army khaki green, and the lighter tone a light yellow green. However, the combination of the dark green body and wings with the light green underwing and body moulding, together with the tan hood and trunk and cream interior, on this body style is perfection. In the days of the custom body builder, the colour scheme was an integral part of the whole design, which is not so well understood in these days of the mass car market, as we saw

OPPOSITE PAGE:
TOP: Interior detail of the Doc Elsner Duesenberg.
BOTTOM: Doc Elsner's 1933 Derham Tourster Duesenberg at home.

THIS PAGE:
RIGHT: 'J-231' 1933 Rollston Convertible Victoria Duesenberg with full engine and chassis detail in one-fifteenth scale.
BELOW: 'J-504' 1933 Derham Tourster Duesenberg with full engine and chassis detail in one-fifteenth scale.

LEFT: 'J-448' 1931 Derham Tourster Duesenberg with a modern two-tone colour scheme.

BELOW: 'J-431' 1929 Derham Tourster Duesenberg, with an original two-tone colour scheme, formerly owned by Gary Cooper.

with the big Bugatti. The Derham Tourster is another case in point; 'J-448' is a modern colour scheme of orange and black, which totally ignores the purpose of the body moulding. On the other hand, 'J-431', with its yellow and light green, is an original colour scheme, and although the treatment is different from 'J-504', it does honour the principle of this style of body moulding, being used simply as a contrasting band for pin-striping. More will be said on this particular car later.

I had been corresponding with Doc for about a year, and he was very enthusiastic about our project to build a fully detailed miniature of a 'J' Duesenberg. He had sent me numerous photos of his car and invited us out to see it and photograph it for ourselves, an invitation that one just could not turn down in my state of mind. The Duesey for me had become heaven on earth. On arrival at Doc's extensive and rambling house in Crete, we were immediately taken to the four-car garage and there it stood, together with some other goodies of the period. He quickly fired it up, our cases having been dumped down by the garage door and we were invited to 'climb' in (it is a big car). We drove down the narrow gravel drive while he narrated to us that the previous week he had nearly drowned in the large lake close by our offside wheels, when his tractor had slipped off the drive into the lake and nearly trapped him under it. About 20 miles out on the open road, he stopped and insisted that I take the wheel. Having only driven once before, just two days previously, on the 'wrong side' (to the English eye) of the road in the USA, I was, to say the least, extremely reluctant, but he would not hear my protestations, and so we exchanged seats. After a little education as to which pedal did what, and what one needed to do with that ever-so-long gear-change lever, we were on our way back. I found the car a joy to drive, though I probably would have done no matter what, but it did not feel at all as big as it looked, nor was the steering heavy (power steering was still a novelty at home at this time), and the big seven-litre engine ran with a low hum. That was until Doc reached down between his legs, where, just in front of his seat, was a short lever that he proceeded to flick over. At that, we heard a fair rumble from the rear as the eight-cylinder engine exhausted itself on to the open road without a silencer. This is a feature on several of the big cars of the period, a sound that is sure to turn heads, but would not be allowed today. Great fun was had by all and I did negotiate that gravel drive without going into the lake. No sooner back, than he was out and into his next masterpiece, an original supercharged Auburn Speedster. This time I was not given a demonstration; I had to drive it out and back to the house. These memories will stay with me always.

We accepted our first Duesenberg order from Doc Elsner for a miniature of his car, and he later ordered a miniature of the chassis and another of the engine, and he would take all three packed in boxes in the back of the car whenever he took the Duesey to shows and meetings, which he did several times a year. In 1979, in an article in *Bulb Horn* (Veteran Motor Car Club of America Inc. Journal), Bart M. Crook wrote:

> I had my experience on the 1976 Glidden Tour. I had the good fortune to meet a Dr C.H. Elsner of Crete, Nebraska, driving a superb 1933 Duesenberg Derham Tourster. It was while at a morning coffee stop I observed the good Doctor exhibiting to a crowd of startled onlookers an exact one-fifteenth scale model of the car he was driving ... When I informed Doc Elsner that I desired to do extensive photography of both his Duesenberg and his model and perhaps an article, he granted me a full morning and a ride in his magnificent motorcar to Colorado Springs' 'Garden of the Gods', where I acquired my needed photos.
>
> Something fascinating came to my attention while travelling that morning in Doc Elsner's Duesenberg. The model was resting on the floorboards by my feet and as the real car would experience a bump in the road, the model would react in what appeared to be a direct relation to its size. The model's suspension reaction was a 'thing of beauty'.

OPPOSITE PAGE:
'SJ-548' Walker La Grande Torpedo Phaeton Duesenberg with full engine and chassis detail in one-fifteenth scale.

THIS PAGE:
LEFT: 'SJ-496' 1932 Brunn Torpedo Phaeton Duesenberg.
BELOW: 'J-550', a beautiful 1933 long wheelbase Convertible Coupé by Rollston of New York.

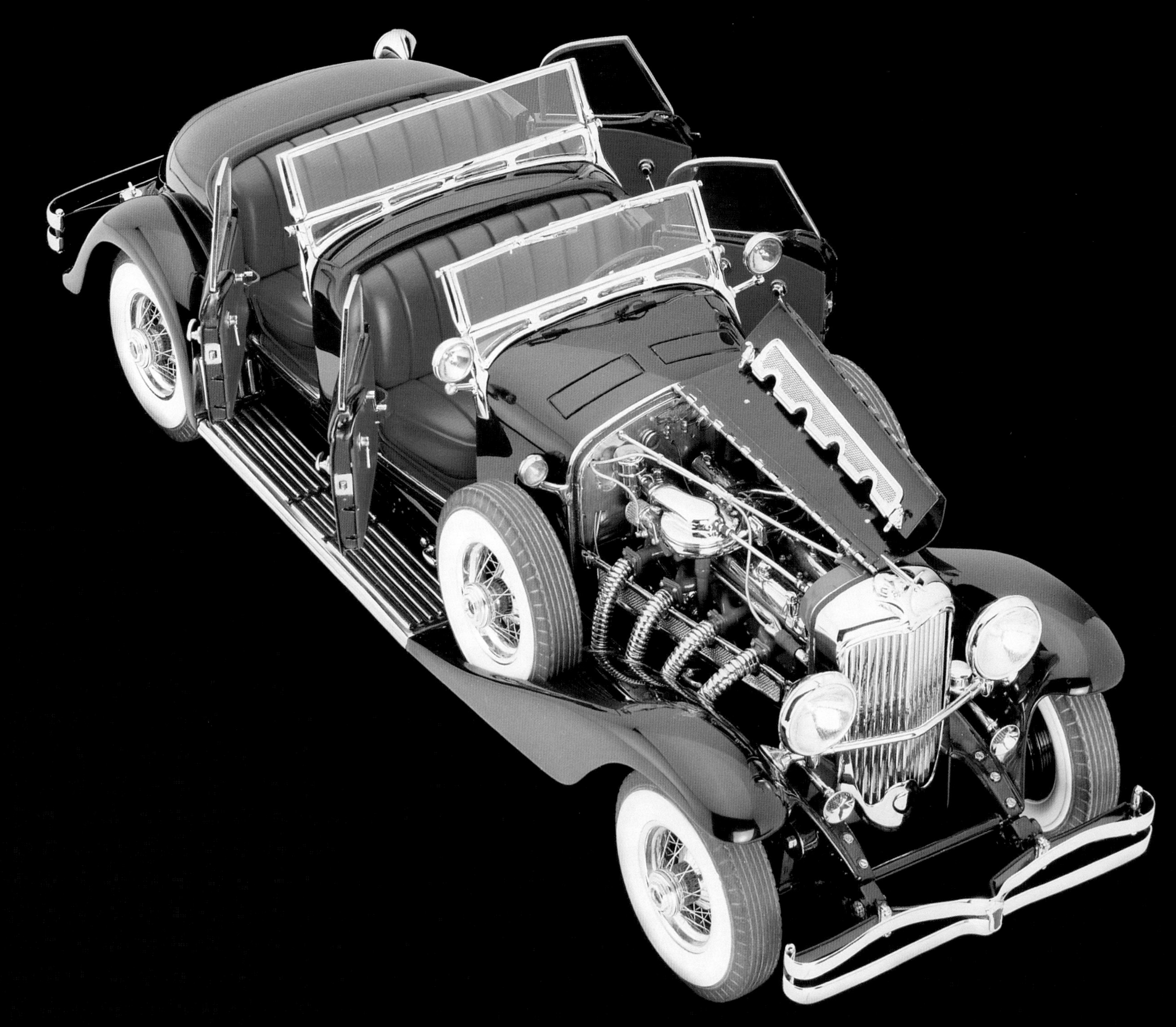

ABOVE LEFT: Murphy Duesenberg 'J-120' on the work-bench, ready for paint and plating.

ABOVE: 'J-120' Murphy Boat Tailed Speedster Duesenberg.

LEFT: Murphy Boat Tailed Speedster Duesenberg, showing engine detail, one-fifteenth scale.

I should say here that just two models were made with spring steel leaf springs so that they actually worked. Experience has taught me that showing a model with working suspension can sometimes result in the miniature being bounced up and down as the point is confirmed – not a good state of affairs for an untutored hand on such a fragile piece. Since that time, for this very reason, all leaf springs have been soldered together so that they do not work, and the wheels are threaded on to the axles so that they do not turn.

Two years after our visit to Doc, and collecting the necessary data from his fabulous car, we returned and arranged to meet up in Auburn, Indiana, for the 1975 Auburn Cord Duesenberg Club get-together, an unforgettable event that is always held on the Labor Day weekend each year. The impressive ACD Museum, formerly the offices and showroom from where these cars were actually displayed and sold in the 1930s, and the focal point of the ACD gatherings, had taken Doc's Derham Tourster into the showroom for the Saturday afternoon, to form part of the Museum display. When we arrived with the miniature of his car, they provided a large glass cabinet to display the miniature next to Doc's car. Next to this was a great friend of his, and later to become a great friend to us, signing copies of his book, *Rolling Sculpture*. Gordon M. Buehrig, no less, the original designer of the Derham Tourster 'J' Duesenberg, as well as another dozen fabulous designs for that chassis.

We were introduced and he became fascinated with our work in general, and the miniatures that we created of his designs in particular. At age twenty-five, he had become chief body designer for Duesenberg, makers of one of the most prestigious automobiles in the world. He left in 1936 when the company was closed down, as so many great automobile companies were in the economic depression of the period. Not only did he create some of the most outstanding all-time body designs of the period on the 'J' and 'SJ' Duesenberg chassis, but he also designed the 1935 Auburn Speedster, and, as we have just seen, the 810 series of revolutionary front-wheel-drive Cord cars. As a long-time friend and critic of our work, I valued his complimentary comments above all others, and as the creator of the original designs, we have found no one better qualified to judge our work.

In 1929, when Gordon created the design for the first of the Derham Toursters (eight were eventually built) for the 1930 Salon in the Drake Hotel in Chicago, he chose a pale green for the wings, belt-moulding, interior and steering wheel, and a DuPont colour, Golden Rod, a subdued yellow for the body to match the green. When the body arrived, he was shocked to see it painted in a bright yellow. Apparently the DuPont paint chip had been an obsolete one and they had redesignated the name to a strong vivid yellow. They decided that rather than send it back they would fit it to the chassis to see how it looked – it might just be a show-stopper. After Chicago, the car was sent to the Salon in Los Angeles, where film star Gary Cooper saw it and purchased it. When several years later he learned that Clark Gable had taken delivery of one of the two very short chassis 'SSJ' supercharged Duesenberg Roadsters, Cooper exchanged his Derham Tourster for the other, 'SSJ-563'.

I am very fond of the yellow and green Derham Tourster. To me, it characterized Hollywood and California in the 1930s. However, before we completed the first miniature, I checked with Gordon regarding the original subdued yellow that he had envisaged for the prototype. After checking several samples with him, we made a point of painting the miniature in the colours that he had originally designed for it, and not the bright yellow it was eventually painted. Four miniatures have been completed in this colour scheme.

The very first Duesenberg that attracted my attention was an 'SJ' Convertible Victoria by Rollston ('SJ-517'). This was one of Gordon's favourite designs, and not too far distant from his Gross Point home on the outskirts of Detroit, there resided a sister car (just three were built) whose owner had asked him to see if we would be interested in creating a miniature of it for him. The car, 'J-231' was, at the time, undergoing a ground up restoration, so we were able to collect a good amount of invaluable information before we actually got to see the finished car. It is a fabulous design, but, like so many, not as practical as one would hope, with

FAR LEFT: Presenting Gordon M. Buehrig with a copy of *The Model Cars of Gerald Wingrove*, for which he had written an Introduction, in 1979 outside the ACD Museum.

LEFT: The original Art Deco interior of the ACD Museum in Auburn, Indiana, with a glass case of Wingrove miniatures, at the Labor Day weekend in 1989.

BELOW LEFT: Gordon at eighty-five shaking hands with our daughter, Alexandra, and about to drive off in his Corvette Stingray, an inspiration never to grow old.

BELOW: Discussing Duesenberg miniatures with Gordon in 1994.

one enormous door on each side; so long, in fact, that it accommodates a door handle at each end, and when both are open they look like wings. The full name for this body design is a Torpedo Convertible Victoria.

Another fabulous Torpedo design from the master's hand (I do not apologize for repeating these words) is 'SJ-496', the Brunn Torpedo Duel Cowl Phaeton. Four similar bodies were built by other makers, one of which, 'SJ-526' body by La Grande, we have also created in miniature, but all have very subtle differences to the shape of the curves over the rear body, and on the tops of the doors up to the screen. The most perfect is the Brunn (two miniatures have been built), which also sports the original eight-into-one exhaust pipe out of the side of the bonnet. Only six cars were ever fitted with this exhaust system, designed for the supercharged cars, as it was apparently apt to glow red when power was applied to an engine that now developed some 320bhp, propelling the car up to 104mph (167km/h) in second gear and 130mph (209km/h) in top. Later, supercharged cars were fitted with the more familiar four large outside exhaust pipes. In the 1930s, these were also offered as a standard accessory for those who wished to appear to be driving a supercharged car, and Doc's car had been modified in this way. Some original photos show it fitted with the curved louvred side panels to the bonnet of a standard 'J' Duesenberg.

A more recent design, that I also consider outstanding and illustrates perfectly 'Automotive Art', is 'J-120', the Murphy Boat-Tailed Speedster; or, as described in the factory literature of the time, the 'Disappearing Top Convertible Coupé'. Six cars of this design were originally built, but only one, this example, was fitted on a long wheelbase chassis, which allows for better proportions. The body, wing and interior are black, while the bonnet moulding and rear deck are polished aluminium. The set of curved side louvres have also been replaced with eight small chromed rectangular doors. The miniature, just one made to date, was a pleasure to build, and was particularly well received when delivered to its new home, which also housed the full-size car. The car was built in 1933 for George Whittell, who placed orders with Duesenberg in the early 1930s for no fewer than six very distinctive cars.

Another of his cars was 'SJ-508', the Fish Tail Speedster by Weymann, built for the 1933 New York Automobile Show. This is a two-seater body built on a long wheelbase chassis, and although it looks very odd with the hood up, it is breathtaking with it down and out of sight, under the rear deck behind the seats. The colour is black and white, with black interior, but with an under-wing colour of bright red, flashes of which show themselves as one walks around the car, or as it speeds past. The wheels are the standard Duesenberg wire-spoked variety, but with spun and ribbed discs attached. The exhaust system is one of a kind, in that a special manifold takes the bottoms of the four outside exhaust pipes to the silencer in such a way that they are all parallel with each other. George Whittell owned a vast amount of land in Nevada and California around Lake Tahoe, part of which was given over to another of his passions, wild animals, which included deer, giraffe, hippopotamus, cheetahs and lions. It is reported that he could often be seen driving around the area with one of his pet lion cubs in the Weymann Speedster. Fred Roe in his book, *Duesenberg, The Pursuit of Perfection*, quotes Mr Whittle as saying that, 'it looked so fast even when going slowly, that he was often getting stopped', which is probably the reason why it only had 13,000 miles on the clock when 'The Harrah's Collection' acquired it from him in the 1950s. Nine miniatures have been built of this subject, six of which have full engine and chassis detail.

The Duesenberg was not just a pretty face. The Duesenberg brothers Fred and Augie had established for themselves a fine reputation as designers and builders of racing cars in the 1920s, culminating internationally when a Duesenberg race car won the French Grand Prix at Le Mans in 1921. In 1935, a standard long wheelbase chassis ('SJ-557') was used with a slightly modified 'SJ' engine to set thirty-six speed and distance records, including twenty-four hours at an average speed of 135.47mph (217.97km/h), with one lap timed at over 160mph (257km/h). In all, we have built forty-one miniatures of 'J' and 'SJ' Duesenbergs, with all but three having full engine and chassis detail.

The fabulous Weymann Fish Tail Speedster 'SJ' Duesenberg.

La Grande Roadster supercharged engine detail.

Briggs Cunningham taking delivery of a miniature of his 'SSJ' La Grande Roadster, in front of the actual car.

Ex-Gary Cooper 'SSJ' Duesenberg La Grande Roadster.

OPPOSITE: 1935 'SSJ-563' Duesenberg La Grande Roadster, with full engine and chassis detail in one-fifteenth scale.

1963 Ferrari 250 GTO

OPPOSITE: 1963 Ferrari 250 GTO with engine detail, built to a scale of one-fifteenth.

THE 1964 250 GTO WAS THE FIRST SUBJECT THAT I BUILT IN ONE-FIFTEENTH scale; the client wanted something a little larger than the one-twentieth scale that I had been working in at that time, and also requested engine detail. I was delighted to have been asked to make the miniature and was quite thrilled at building a Ferrari, a name that has always conjured up a spirit of excitement. The data was collected, the plans drafted and the building started (Ferrari enthusiasts should probably read no further), but then something occurred that has never happened with any other subject – I was unable to maintain the necessary focused attention required for this sort of work, and would find myself wandering around the garden when I should have been at the workbench.

The 250 GTO series of cars made an outstanding name for themselves and Ferrari in 1963 and 1964, and the cars, both full size and miniature, are coveted above all others by a large group of collectors. However, for me the aesthetics of the design just do not work, particularly the angle of the windscreen, which distracts me no end. Like the E-Type Jaguar, I think it is much too steep and completely destroys the whole concept of a speed machine. To recreate anything in miniature, I have to look at it for twelve hours a day for seven days a week, for three months or more, and if I am not happy with it as a design, I find great difficulty in reaching its character, and, for me, this is where the problem lay.

Although we have been continually asked to make miniatures of these by collectors in Europe, the USA and Japan, we never have returned to them. Of the six built, five have opening doors with working door catches and a bonnet that opens from a latch under the dashboard, as on the full-size car. These have engine detail as seen through the bonnet, but no chassis or underbody detail. One other was built as a curbside miniature without opening side doors or bonnet and no engine detail.

Ferrari 250 GTO engine detail.

1963 Ferrari 250 GTO.

MLS 1

1913 Model 'T' Ford

OPPOSITE: 1913 Model 'T' Ford with Runabout body, having full engine and chassis detail built to a scale of one-fifteenth.

IN 1972, SHORTLY AFTER BUILDING THE FERRARI MINIATURES, I ACCEPTED a commission to build a Model 'T' Ford for a display in the Evoluon Museum in Holland. I located three cars, and collected the data for the plans, and ordered several books on the subject. The museum requirement was for an open four-seater, but without engine or underbody detail. Even without engine detail, cars of this period showed plenty of chassis parts, so a more or less fully detailed set of plans was required. They were also looking for a reasonable size of model and the one-fifteenth scale was accepted.

One of the books I obtained was *Henry's Wonderful Model 'T' 1908–1927* by Floyd Clymer, which is full of old photos and anecdotes about the cars, their owners and the times in which they were the mainstay of popular transport in the USA. In particular, they were used on the farms for just about everything. The car became a way of life affectionately known as 'The Tin Lizzie', and less affectionately known as 'Henry's Heap'. It was the comedy car of the early films, associated with such names as The Keystone Cops and Laurel and Hardy, the butt of endless jokes, cartoons, stories, both fact and fiction, and poets and song-writers had a field day with it. No other car in history had such an impact and there were some fifteen million built with only minor detail changes, until production stopped in May 1927.

Seeing the car and reading the stories got me hooked; it resembled every bit of its history, time, place and culture, and the little two-seater 'Runabout', as it was listed in the 1913 catalogue (well, not so little, as the folding hood can be a good 6 feet off the ground), epitomized it all. The four-seater was built for the museum as a curbside model with no engine detail, but three others, with the Runabout two-seater body, folding hood and full engine and chassis detail were also created, together with one fully detailed chassis. Another attraction of this as a subject was its being the complete opposite of the 'J' Duesenberg – a car for the masses compared to the one for the very wealthy. They look very interesting standing side by side, each designed for a purpose and showing it in every part.

1913 'Tin Lizzie' Model 'T' Ford Runabout.

Hispano Suiza H6C

OPPOSITE: 1924 Hispano Suiza H6C fully planked and pinned, with engine and chassis detail in one-fifteenth scale.

THIS CAR HAS BEEN FEATURED IN HUNDREDS OF BOOKS ON CLASSIC CARS over the past fifty years, under the erroneous heading of 'The Tulipwood Car'. Together with countless journalists and writers on automobile topics, I too had read it somewhere and repeated it, on the presumption that it got its name from the body having been built from tulipwood, an exotic Brazilian hardwood. Roy Middleton and my own curiosity got the better of us when a large question mark was put on this, and the car turned out to have been built of a somewhat less exotic timber – Honduras mahogany. However, let us start at the beginning.

On receiving a phone call one day from a collector who had just taken delivery of this car, he asked me if I would like to build him a miniature of it. Having known of the car for many years (there is only one in existence and it was on my 'want-to-make-sometime' list), I grabbed my camera and notebook, jumped in my car, and was halfway to his place before he could put his phone down. Seeing the car in the flesh for the first time takes your breath away – the sheer size of it, almost 20 feet long with all those rivets. What had I let myself in for?

Standing there with the owner, we surveyed its beauty and discussed what sort of a miniature it would make. I suggested that the polished woodwork might look better on the miniature if it did not have all the pins in it, but my client would not hear of it; all the rivets must be included, he declared. With a little discussion, we settled on a miniature complete in every detail. I was slightly worried, though, for I could see that if the rivets were not almost as thin as a hair on a 15-inch long model, then the finish would be more akin to that of an old nail-studded oak door.

Arriving back at my workshop I made up a small sample of bodywork, planked it and pinned it, then stained and polished it to match the colour samples I had brought back with me from the car. A set of scale plans was drafted from the dimensions and photographs that had been collected, and with the drawings and sample, I returned north to meet again with the owner and, happily, all was favourably accepted. The miniature would be planked in pear wood (a very closed grained hardwood), to give a scale grain effect and stained to match the full-size car. The rivets would be represented by short pins of brass wire just twelve-thousandths of an inch in diameter; I later estimated that there were probably in the order of 13,000 pins (rivets) on a miniature with the wood-planked pontoon wings. Like drilling spoke holes, this is a task that one has to prepare oneself for, usually with a good selection of Mozart and Beethoven CDs at full volume to put the mind on to another plane.

When it comes to fitting the tiny brass pins in place, I must admit that it has often been a case of offering a bribe to daughter Alexandra to help out Phyllis in what

1924 Hispano Suiza H6C as it appeared in the 1960s.

must be the most tedious task of all our model engineering. However, when all is cleaned up and French polished, the finished results must be the most stunning body finish of all our miniatures. As there is a full-length undertray, albeit in sections, from the radiator right back to the tail cone, and the top half of the engine crankcase is cast integrally with a sort of tray on each side that blocks off the lower part of the engine casing and sump, it was agreed that only the top half of the engine, visible with the bonnet open, need be made.

The car had gone though a lot of changes in its life, even to having the wheels and some of the brightwork copper-plated, presumably to match the red of the woodwork in some way. This had taken on an odd tone, and I made the point that in all of the book illustrations that I had seen, this copper work looked in fact more like old gold, so why not have these parts gold-plated on the miniature so they that would never need cleaning? The owner was so taken with the idea that he said that if or when he restored the car, he would consider having these parts gold-plated as well to match the miniature. He placed an order for two miniatures, and shortly after taking delivery of them, he sold the car, so it never did get the gold treatment.

Although looking nothing like the car as originally built, at that particular time the Hispano Suiza looked like a grand old lady, with a finish to the woodwork that an antique dealer would love. Unfortunately, in my opinion, this grand old lady has, in recent years, suffered the most dreadful of rebuilds – it would be sacrilegious to call it a restoration. Gone is the salmon/buff-painted aluminium undertray, replaced by polished sheet copper. Gone is the brown-piped, dove-grey interior, replaced with a bright cream leather. Gone is the weather-worn and coloured copper plating of the wheels and brightwork, replaced with saucepan-bright new shining copper plate. Everything that could be plated in the engine compartment has been chrome-plated, and gone is the beautiful antique finish to the woodwork, which has been scraped back to bare boards and finished in what for all the world looks like a modern polyurethane varnish.

OPPOSITE: 1924 Hispano Suiza H6C as it appeared at the end of 1924, with engine and chassis detail in one-fifteenth scale.

This machine started life as a Grand Prix car for André Dubonnet (of aperitif fame) to race in the 1924 Targo Florio, where he finished sixth, racing against the factory teams of Mercedes, Alfa, Fiat and Itala. The wooden body was created by Nieuport Astra, a notable French First World War aircraft manufacturer, which used its expertise to produce a very lightweight body structure of laminated wood. Several French motor-body builders, notably the Henri-Labourdette Carrosserie of Paris, used similar techniques on a wide range of body styles at this time, to produce some very interesting designs. The system consisted of a very light framework of closely spaced ribs, across which were secured narrow strips of very thin wood at an angle of 45 degrees to the ribs. If two layers were to be used, the second would be set opposite to the first. If three, then the third

1924 Hispano Suiza H6C as it appeared at the end of 1925, with engine and chassis detail in one-fifteenth scale.

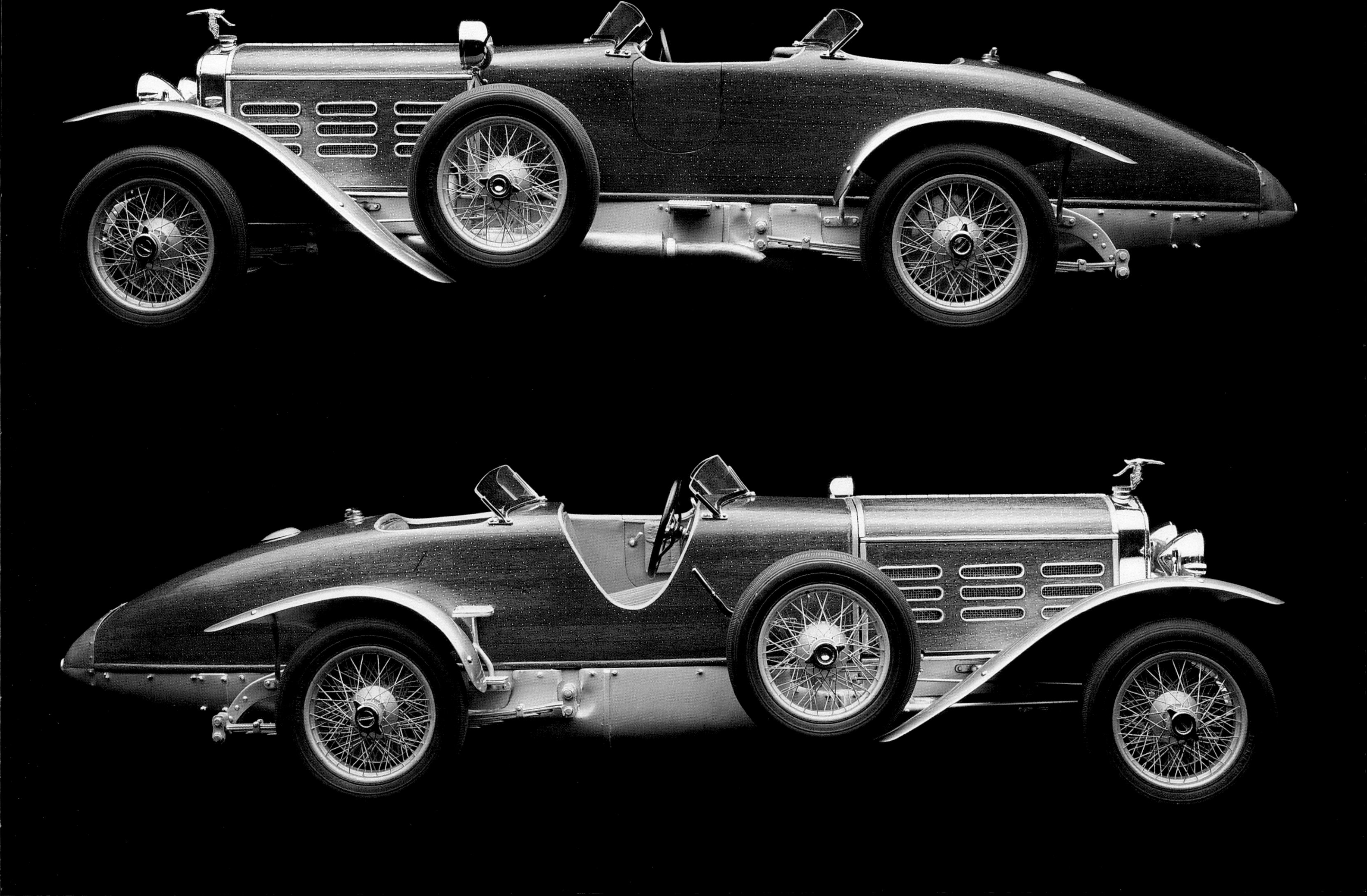

would be horizontal, as in this case. Rivets would then be spaced along the length of the planking to secure it permanently to the ribs.

The Hispano Suiza originally appeared and raced without wings; however, there is a photograph of the car taken at the Nieuport Astra works showing it fitted with headlights, a large spotlight mounted on the left side of the cowl just back from the firewall, and small, swept wings front and rear. These, together with the undertray, appear to be aluminium and unpainted. The wheels are light grey in the photos (black and white), which I have taken to be silver, and so have painted the miniatures created to represent the car at this time. In 1925, the car came to England and was photographed at the Brooklands racetrack in the spectators' enclosure. This now shows the wheels, wings and undertray to be very dark, which I have interpreted as black in the miniatures that show it at this period. The wings have also been replaced with slightly larger ones, and the rear stays for the rear wings have the brackets in place for the luggage rack. Both the 1924 and 1925 photos show small neat 'V' windscreens to the front and rear cockpits.

From the late 1930s to 1950, the car was in storage at a warehouse belonging to the coachbuilders Hoopers, on the King's Road in London. It was discovered there by Rodney Forester-Walker, who then purchased the car. By this time, the swept wings were missing, so he had a set of small cycle-type wings made and fitted, and used the car for the next five years. In 1956, the car was seen parked in a London street by Gerald Albertini, who left a note attached to the steering wheel to the effect that should the owner ever decide to sell, please to let him know. Several weeks later, after considerable negotiation, Gerald Albertini became the new owner. He undertook some restoration and, disliking the cycle wings, he had the pontoon wings built around them by a Thames boatbuilder, and this is what we see today. In the next decade, the car crossed the Atlantic several times, and it was on one of its comparatively short stays in English ownership that I was invited to create the first miniatures. At the time of writing, it resides in a large car collection in California.

I described the building of the first miniature in my book on car modelling, *The Complete Car Modeller*, on the cover of which is a large colour photograph of the miniature Hispano Suiza, with wood planked and pinned bodywork. In Potters Bar, North London, lived an enthusiastic Hispano Suiza owner, Roy Middleton, who not only had a very fine K6 Hispano with Cabriolet bodywork by Fernandez that he had already restored and used widely on rallies across Europe, but he also owned an H6 Hispano chassis, complete with engine and running gear. In the early 1990s, his wife Tania was looking for a Christmas present for him, and knowing he was interested in all things Hispano, chanced upon my book with the Hispano picture on the cover, and purchased it for him. In

ABOVE: Brazilian tulipwood block showing the 'blip' in the annual rings.

RIGHT: Tulipwood being sliced on a milling machine, ready for splitting into one-fifteenth scale planks.

the back of the book was a copy of the set of plans from which the miniature had been made.

A year or so prior to this, a BBC television documentary programme was made on our work, some of which was filmed in the workshop. The MD of a large importer of machine tools happened to see the programme and noted that all of our machines were the imported products of his company. He suggested that we might work together by showing our work as examples of what could be made on his machine tools. Thus started a long association, the highlight of which was the annual get-together at The Model Engineering Exhibition in London. The exhibition would last for a week and I would attend the first and last days to deliver and collect the miniatures on loan at the time. I happened to be on the exhibition stand one Saturday and noticed this gentleman scrutinizing the model collection. He would disappear for an hour or so, but then return again for another ten minutes of close examination. Late in the afternoon, I introduced myself and inquired as to his particular interest, which turned out to be the miniature of the Hispano Suiza H6C with polished aluminium wings in the glass case. I was astonished to learn that he was in the process of building a full-size replica body of this car from my original scale model plans from the back of the book. Not only that, but he had photographically enlarged the plans and noted that his radiator was one and a half inches higher than I had shown, and so had taken his original one apart and shortened it to match!

Thus started a fascinating friendship with Roy Middleton, who had an exceptional talent for engineering. When he later visited us to have a closer look at our work, I presented him with copies of all of the data and photographs that we had collected on this car. During the next several years, whenever we were in North London, we visited him and admired his splendid work as his recreation took shape. His aim was not to make an exact copy of the original, which had been designed as a GP car, but to use the original as inspiration and to correct its shortcomings, not least of which was its very narrow and cramped seating accommodation.

His method of building differed considerably from the original, being taken more from modern boatbuilding practice than First World War fighter aircraft production. Several bulkheads were secured across the chassis frame, over which were placed lengths of one-inch square mahogany. These were trimmed and glued together to form a solid shell. On to this was attached, with very great skill using modern adhesives, strips of veneer. It was at this stage that the questions started to come thick and fast, with phone calls several times a week on my knowledge of timbers, of which I have a very large collection. The problem was that Roy had been making his own collection of tulipwood veneers and trying to match them to the timber on the actual car. I had supplied him with several colour photographs, but he was not having much success. The difficulty was that all of his samples of tulipwood were figured with red and cream banding, about as far removed from the antique-furniture tone of the car as it was possible to get. He then received an invitation to show his K6 Hispano at a motor show in Germany, and learned that the original H6C ex-Dubonnet car was being flown over from the States for the same show. With this information, he enlisted the help of a timber expert to visit the car in Germany and establish exactly what timber the body was constructed from. He told me afterwards that on visiting the car with the expert, he spotted it from a hundred feet away and informed him that it had to be of Honduras mahogany, and on closer examination this was confirmed.

By this time, Roy had become very fond of the exotic Brazilian tulipwood timber that he had discovered and the thought occurred to him, 'Wouldn't it be great fun actually to have the only truly tulipwood-finished Hispano Suiza in the world?' The decision was made, the veneers ordered and a specialist company with the necessary vacuum equipment to secure them to the body shell was found. The intention was to simulate the rivet heads and the pattern of them on the new body; however, when the body was returned sanded and finished with a clear polish, he was so thrilled with it that he decided to leave well alone. By this time, he had made a full set of swept wings in aluminium and polished them

1980 Replicar and 1924 original miniatures ready for planking.

Planking the pontoon fenders for the 1960s miniature.

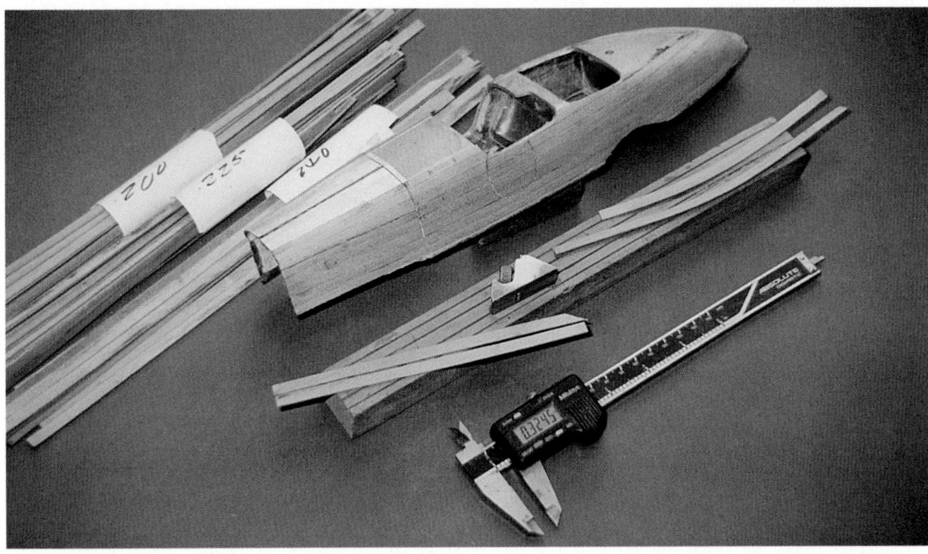

1924 miniature being planked with pear wood to simulate mahogany.

1980 Replicar miniature being planked with Brazilian tulipwood.

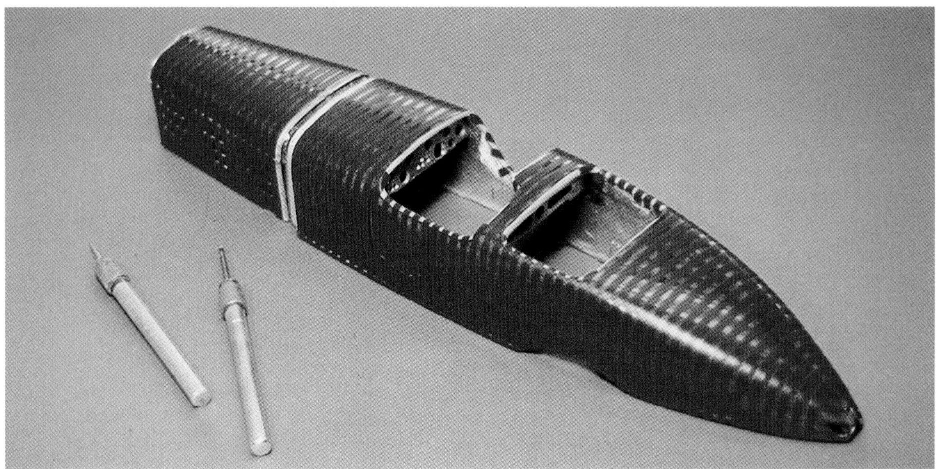

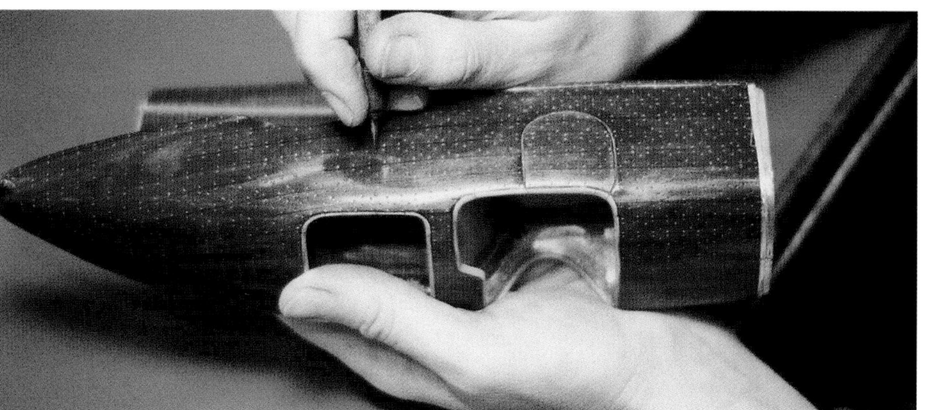

ABOVE: 1924 scale body banded with tape at the simulated frame rib positions to mark out for drilling the rivet (pin) holes.

ABOVE RIGHT: Centring the rivet (pin) holes.

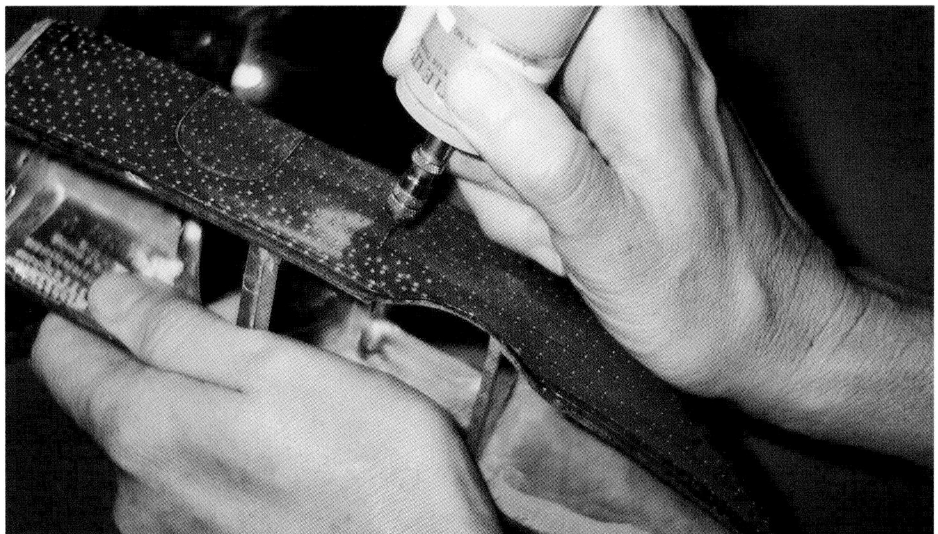

ABOVE: Drilling the twelve-thousandths of an inch diameter rivet (pin) holes.

RIGHT: Daughter Alexandra fitting the pins (rivets) in place.

The 1924 (top) and 1980 (bottom) one-fifteenth scale miniatures, planked and pinned (1924 only) ready for painting and plating.

to a very high finish, for it was the model that we had built showing the first set of swept wings that had really attracted him. The last time we visited Roy, the car was all but complete, with aluminium undertray and front apron, needing only the wheels to be painted silver and the interior fitted out in dark red leather.

About six months later we learned to our great dismay that Roy had died; we had lost a good friend and were so sorry that he did not get to see his project finished and to drive it on the open road. The car was passed to a specialist company to be completed and we lost track of it. About three years later, we received an enquiry from someone who wanted us to build a miniature as a birthday present, and the car was the Tulipwood Hispano Suiza recently acquired by her husband. We arranged to see the car, and there it was, Roy Middleton's creation. However, it was nothing like its former self. Those who had finished it to be sold on had not only painted those glorious polished aluminium wings a metallic brown, as well as the wheels and undertray, but had stained the beautiful tulipwood a dark brown as well. We explained to the new owner the shocking things that had been done to his car and with the photos from our last visit to Roy's workshop, illustrated just what an outstanding car it could have been. We were most pleased to learn that, after seeing the car as Roy had designed it, he was considering having the paint and woodwork stripped in due time and put it back to how it would have been finished, and the model should be built to reflect this. We were absolutely delighted to take on the commission, and were able to show in the miniature how we knew Roy wanted to see his car finished.

The new project followed the same build procedure as the other miniatures, except for the planking. There is no way that we could make pear wood take on the amazing cream and red figuring of tulipwood. Veneers of this type are cut from the circumference of a log to produce the type of figuring used on the actual car; however, the timber is of a very fine grain. In my collection of exotic timbers I did have a large block of the wood, which, on examining the end grain, showed an irregularity in the annual rings in the form of a 'blip' that provided the answer I was looking for. If this 'blip' could be sliced very thinly, it could produce a scale figuring for the miniature, although this one 'blip' would hardly supply enough planking for the whole miniature. We found a stockist of small logs of tulipwood, paid him a visit, and after going through a 6-foot-high stack of blocks, I did find another six pieces with similar markings in the annual rings, suitable for producing the required number of planks. These were cut and trimmed so that they could be mounted on a milling machine, and with a very fine engineering slitting saw were cut into sufficient thin strips to cover the scale body. After tapering the ends of each plank with a tiny wood plane to accommodate the rear body curves, these were fixed to the body and bonnet with epoxy resin. The planking was cut to a thickness of about twelve-thousandths of an inch, and after fitting this to the body was later sanded back to a thickness of about an eight-thousandths of an inch, before being finished with a two-part clear acrylic finish, then polished.

The question arises as to how the original Dubonnet car picked up the name 'Tulipwood'. In my very early research into the history of this car, I exchanged a good deal of correspondence with Alec Ulmann, a much respected member of the Hispano Suiza Society, and a fountain of knowledge on all things relevant to the make. Among a large amount of copy that he sent to me was a memorandum on several of these cars, which included the following identification: 'Nieuport tulip type wooden body'. This appeared to have come from a larger document or book, but unfortunately there was not enough of it to identify its origins. I have since checked other sources, some of which indicate a tulip shape, and this, of course, could be applied to the tail end of this car. So it is possible that some journalist, a long time ago, just happened to miss a word out, when he checked on the above description of this car in a long lost book. Instead of a 'Nieuport tulip type wooden body', it went down in his copy as a 'Nieuport tulip wooden body', and was shortened ever after to 'Nieuport tulip wood'. In future, it will be known to me as the ex-Dubonnet Hispano Suiza. In all, we have built thirteen miniatures of the ex-Dubonnet Hispano Suiza and just one of the Tulipwood Hispano Suiza.

1980 Replicar showing tulipwood planked finish.

1924 simulated mahogany (pear wood) and pinned finish.

1980 Tulipwood Replicar body on the 1924 Hispano Suiza H6C chassis.

BELOW: 1924 ex-Dubonnet Hispano Suiza H6C, with the 1980 Roy Middleton Replicar it inspired.

Rolls-Royce 40/50

OPPOSITE: 1912 Rolls-Royce 40/50 with London–Edinburgh touring body 'The Mystery' by Holmes, with full engine and chassis detail in one-fifteenth scale.

IN SEPTEMBER 1911, AN OPEN ROLLS-ROYCE 40/50 TOURER (CHASSIS No. 1701), named the 'Sluggard', took up a challenge from Napier to drive from London to Edinburgh and back using only top gear, the run to be supervised by the RAC. The 65bhp Napier, which had achieved 76mph (122.3km/h) and a fuel consumption of 19.3mpg (14.7ltr/100km), was to be soundly beaten by the 48bhp Rolls-Royce at 78.5mph (126.3km/h) and a fuel consumption of 24mpg (11.8ltr/100km). The total distance travelled by the Rolls-Royce was 794 miles (1,278km). In the following year, the same car, now fitted with a single-seater body, attained a speed of 101mph (163km/h) at Brooklands. The underslung chassis had been an experimental one with cantilever springs to the rear suspension, and it proved so successful that it was adopted for a range of open touring bodies to be called the London–Edinburgh Type.

There were originally fourteen of these cars built, with just five surviving today. This particular example, chassis No. 1826E, being a copy of chassis No. 1701, was built for Claude Johnson, Managing Director of Rolls-Royce, and named 'The Mystery'. It found its way to Australia in 1926, and in 1958 was discovered derelict on a farm in Victoria by a Rolls-Royce enthusiast. In 1976, a three-year restoration was completed and it went on show at the York Motor Museum in Australia. An American collector, Rick Carroll, always on the look-out for important Rolls-Royce cars, heard about it, and in 1986 was able to add it to his own outstanding collection. He considered it of sufficient importance in the history of Rolls-Royce cars to have a ground up restoration undertaken to put it back to as-new condition. We had met Rick Carroll the previous year and had been given a request to build miniatures of all his classic cars, about fifteen in number. After Doc Elsner had passed away he had become the new owner of Duesenberg 'J-504', and that was the first miniature on the list.

The Rolls-Royce 40/50 had been shipped to a specialist Rolls-Royce restoration shop in the UK, where we were invited to collect the necessary data over the next several years. Every assistance was afforded us by the owners of the restoration shop and we would visit it several times a year to photograph firstly the bare chassis frame, then the various components and accessories as they were restored and assembled. Just as the car was in its final stages of completion, and we had collected the last of our photographs and measurements, Rick Carroll tragically died of a heart attack, and his car collection was auctioned by Sotheby's

1912 London–Edinburgh Rolls-Royce 40/50 Tourer 'The Mystery'.

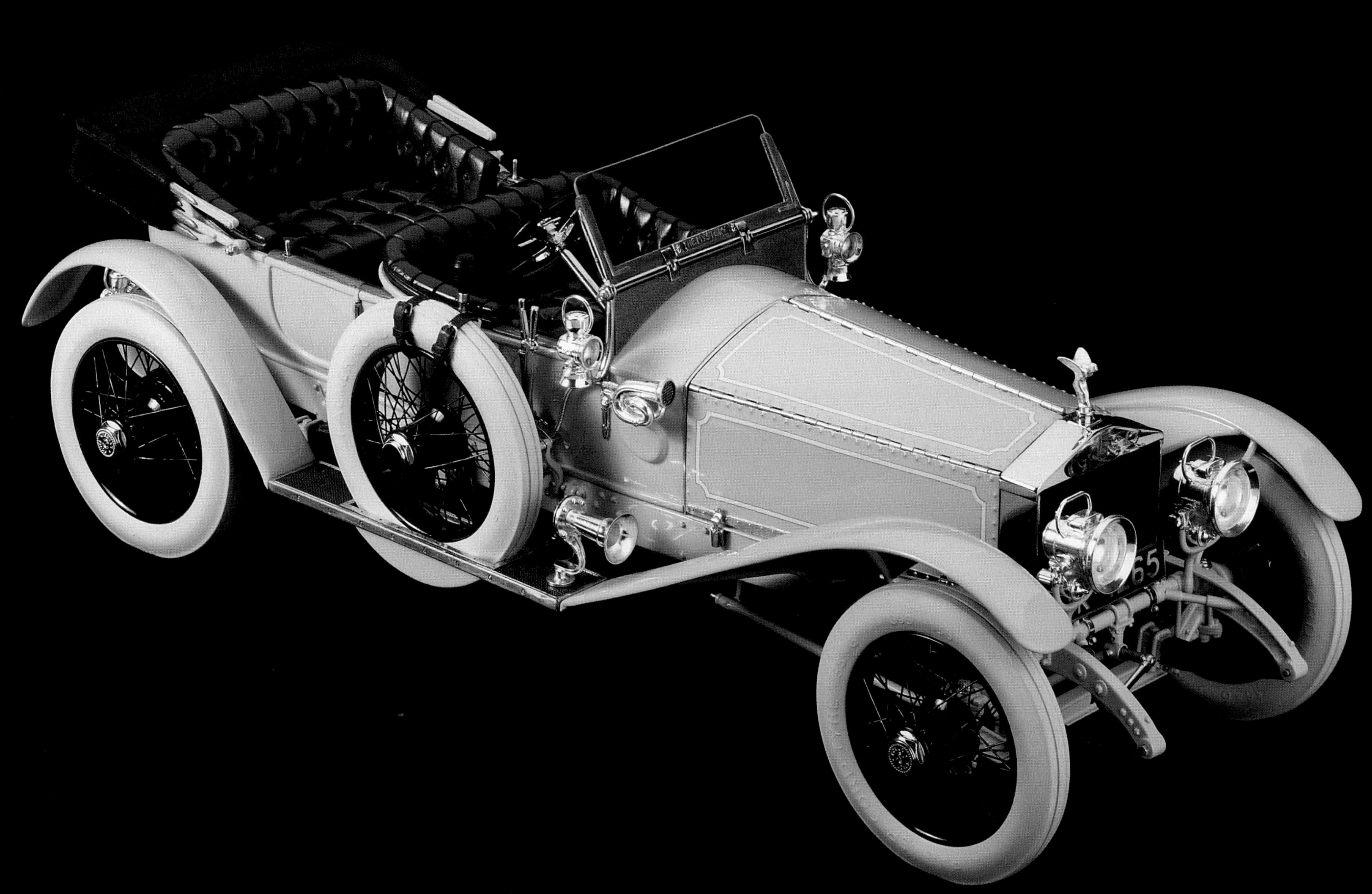

ABOVE LEFT: 1912 40/50 engine in one-fifteenth scale showing inlet side.

ABOVE: Rolls-Royce 40/50 chassis front end showing exhaust side.

LEFT: Rolls-Royce London–Edinburgh Tourer complete and ready for painting and plating.

OPPOSITE: 1912 Rolls-Royce 40/50 chassis complete with full engine detail, wings, lamps, etc., in one-fifteenth scale.

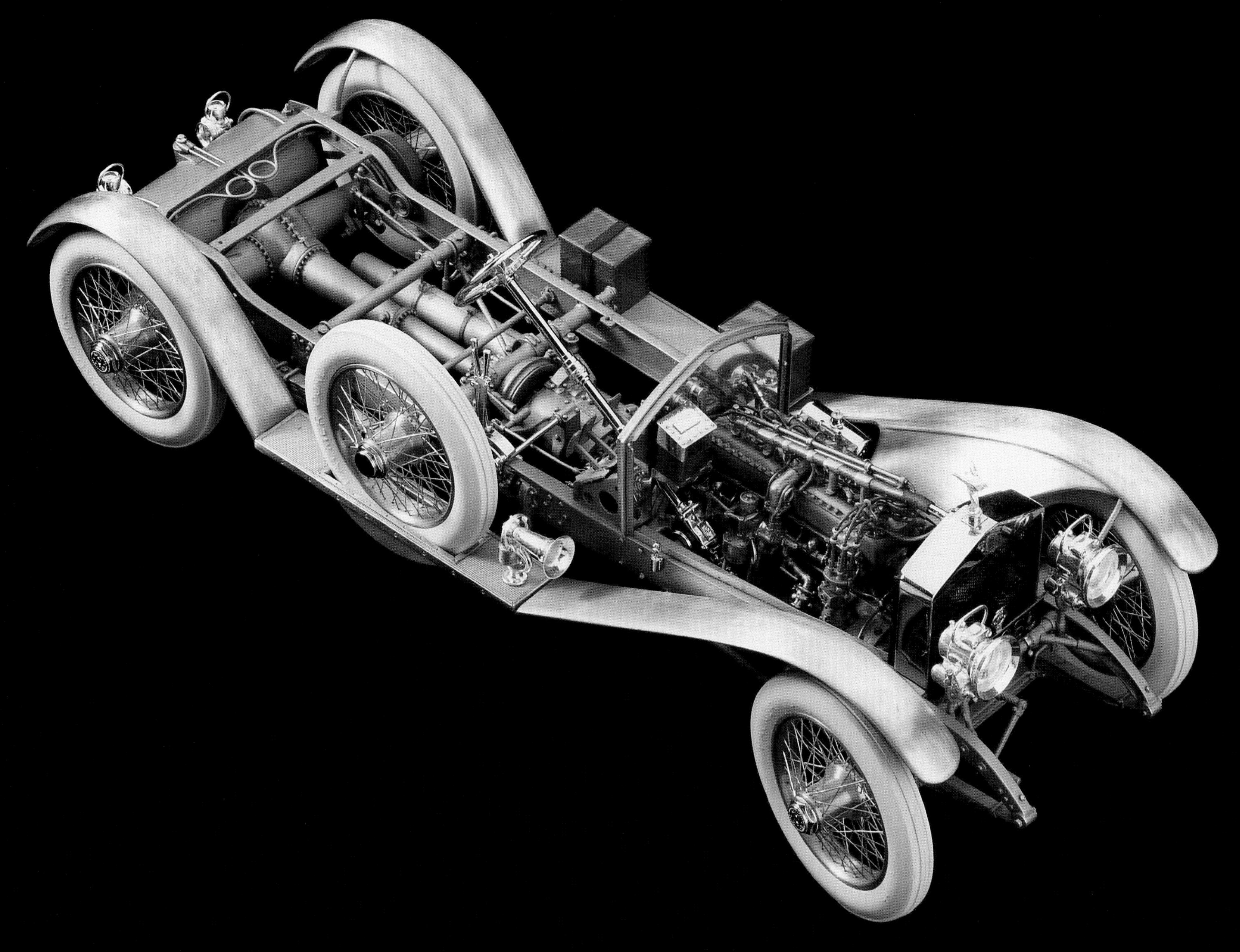

on 12 May 1990. The Duesenberg model that we had started for Rick Carroll was completed and sold to another collector, and the Rolls-Royce 40/50 data and photographs put to the back of the shelf. About two years later, a friend called us from his home in Yorkshire and said that he was driving a colleague down to London airport the following day, and the colleague had asked if he could call by and meet us and see the workshop. This was arranged and the following day they duly arrived to see one of the Weinberger Bugatti Royales nearing completion. The colleague turned out to be the purchaser of 'The Mystery' from the Sotheby's sale, and had a vast collection of the most fabulous cars of his own. He left us with a commission for another miniature of the Weinberger Bugatti Royale and the 1912 Rolls-Royce 40/50. Phyllis now resurrected the Rolls-Royce data and, for the next year, was 'tied' to the Apple Mac drafting the most complicated and detailed set of plans to-date.

I find that many of the body designs fitted to the Rolls-Royce cars of this period are, let's just say, not picturesque, but I suppose if you are going to design a car for someone to get in and out of with a stovepipe hat on, the end result is hardly going to be aerodynamic. However, the underslung 40/50 chassis gave Holmes, the body builder, an ideal platform that they would seem to have taken to heart, for the end result, from its tapered bonnet to its rounded rear end, is perfection in balance, proportion, elegance and English to the core – a work of true automotive art.

The chassis and engine are the most elaborate that we have built, and I was not very far into it when it occurred to me that it was more like boilermaking than building parts for a car. This was not because the parts were big and heavy, but because of the number of bolts used to hold the pieces together. Where most manufacturers would use six bolts to hold a pair of castings together, Messrs Rolls-Royce appeared to use two dozen. With the number of bolts holding the rear-axle castings together, the appearance is more akin to high-pressure steam vessels than a driveshaft and gear housings. It was only after reading the history of the founder members that I learnt that Mr Frederick Henry Royce had served his apprenticeship in the workshops of Great Northern Railways, so perhaps this had left a lasting impression on him. The miniatures, however, were a joy to work on, so tiny and intricate are the parts. The construction followed the usual procedure, excepting that there seemed to be a lot more of it. The brightwork was either nickel- or silver-plated as on the original, and the two boxes on the running boards were assembled from pear wood, and comb-jointed to represent dovetails (on this scale you would be hard put to tell the difference) to the correct number as those on the car. At this time, three miniatures have been created with full engine and chassis detail.

OPPOSITE: 1912 Rolls-Royce 40/50 with London–Edinburgh Touring body showing interior and engine detail in one-fifteenth scale.

Rolls-Royce London–Edinburgh Tourer showing firewall and engine detail.

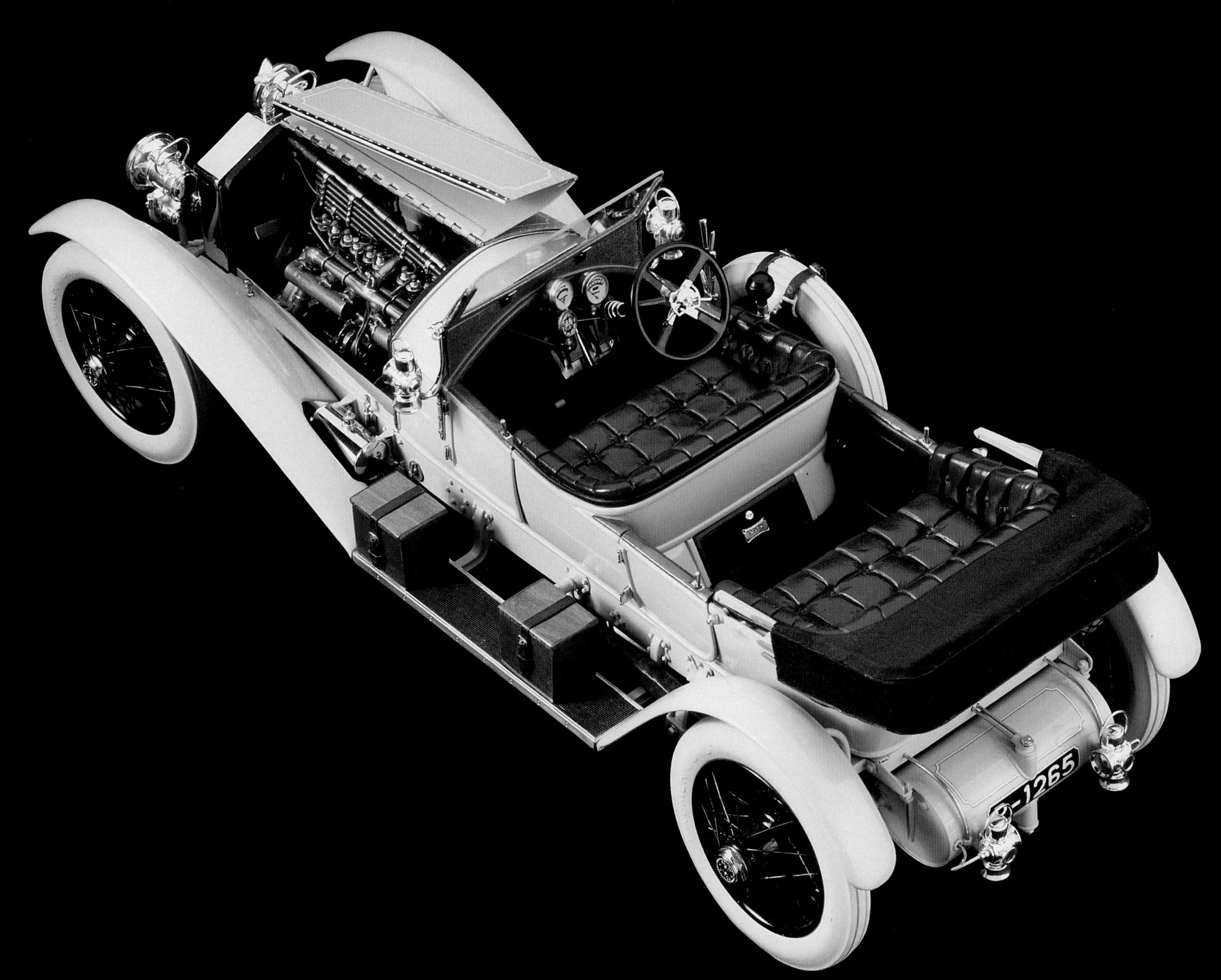
1265

Plans for the 1912 Rolls-Royce 40/50 HP London–Edinburgh Tourer

'THE MYSTERY'

Body by Holmes of Derby
Chassis No. 1826E

Six cylinders in line, cast in two groups of three.
Water-cooled side-valve engine of 7,284 cc.

Bore – 4.5in	Wheelbase – 11ft 11.5in
Stroke – 4.75in	Tyres – 880mm–120mm

The Rolls-Royce plans are typical of those drafted by Phyllis on the Apple Mac computer using Bentley Systems' MicroStation Mac. The information is collected from the actual car by way of notes and dimensions, together with several hundred photographs. The plans shown here are printed to a slightly smaller scale than used to create the miniatures, in order to accommodate them in the space available. The overall length of the Rolls-Royce miniature at one-fifteenth scale is 12½in (318mm).

Copies of the Rolls-Royce plans at a scale of one-fifteenth together with a collection of original data photos of the actual car are available on the internet as portfolios from the 'Wingrove Collection' website at www.wincol.com

---

The end papers are printed at one-fifteenth scale and show the chassis side members for the Bugatti Type 41.

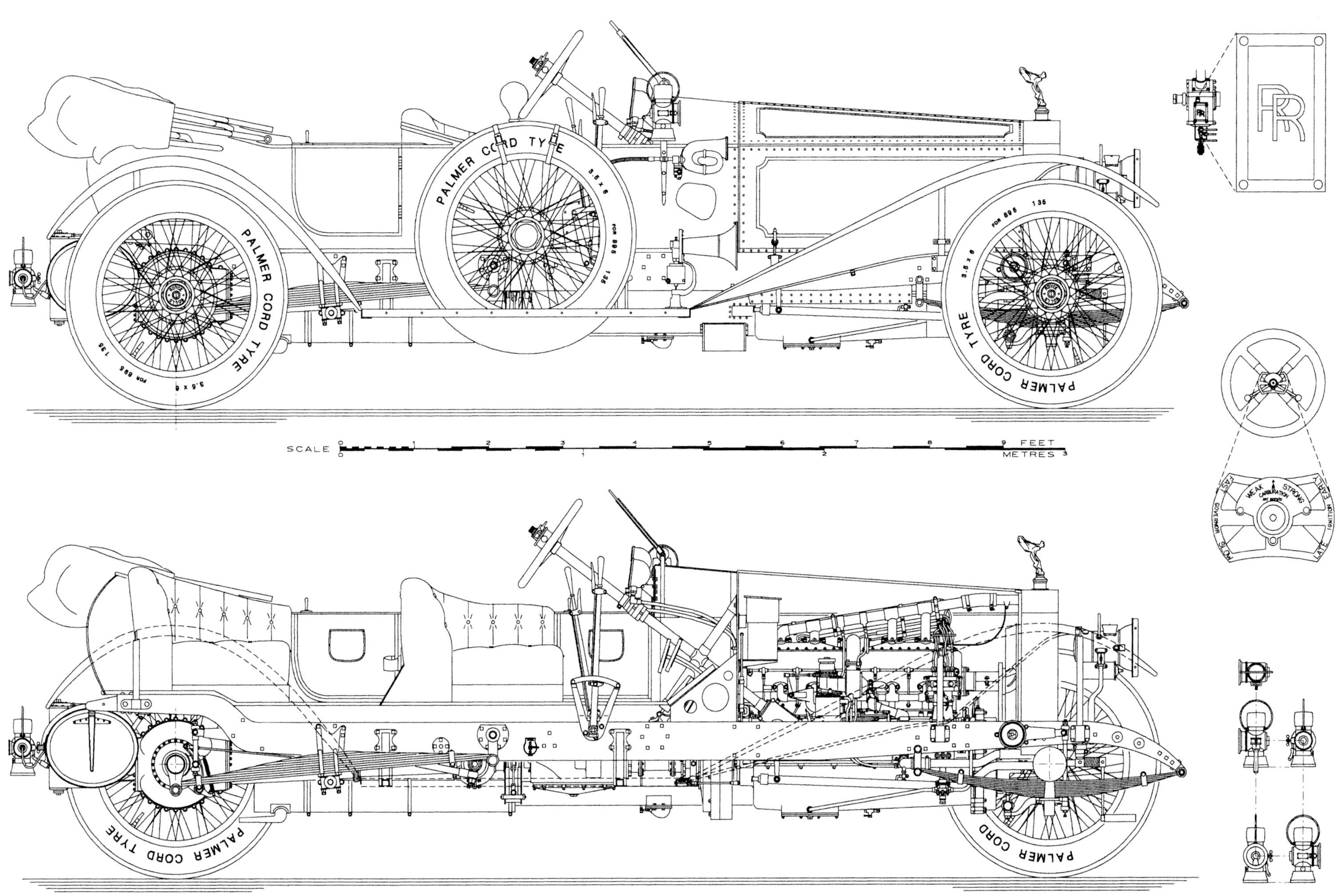

Drafted on Bentley Systems MicroStation©

1912 40/50 Rolls-Royce London-Edinburgh Tourer.

Phyllis & Gerald A Wingrove ©1995

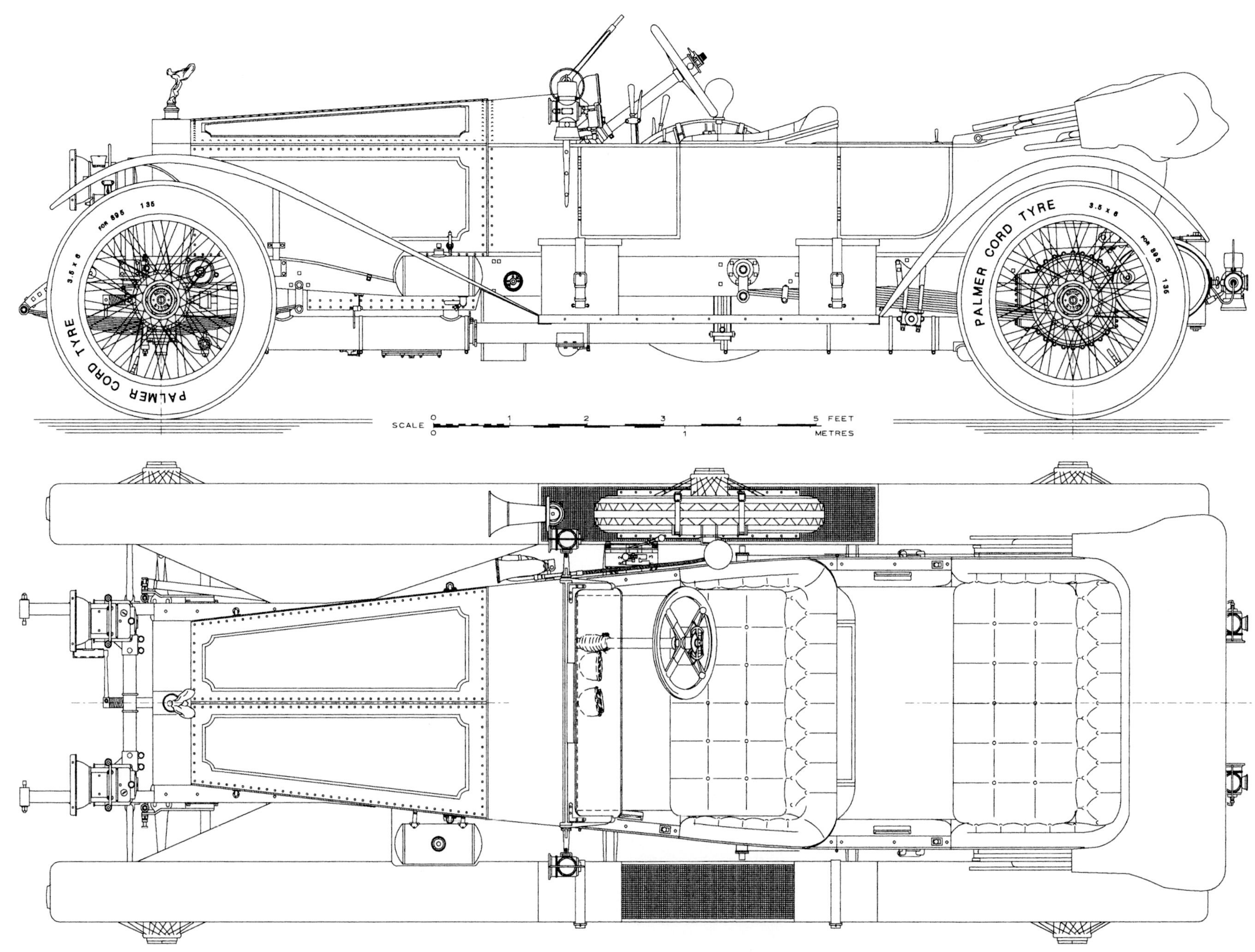

1912 40/50 Rolls-Royce London-Edinburgh Tourer.

Drafted on Bentley Systems MicroStation©

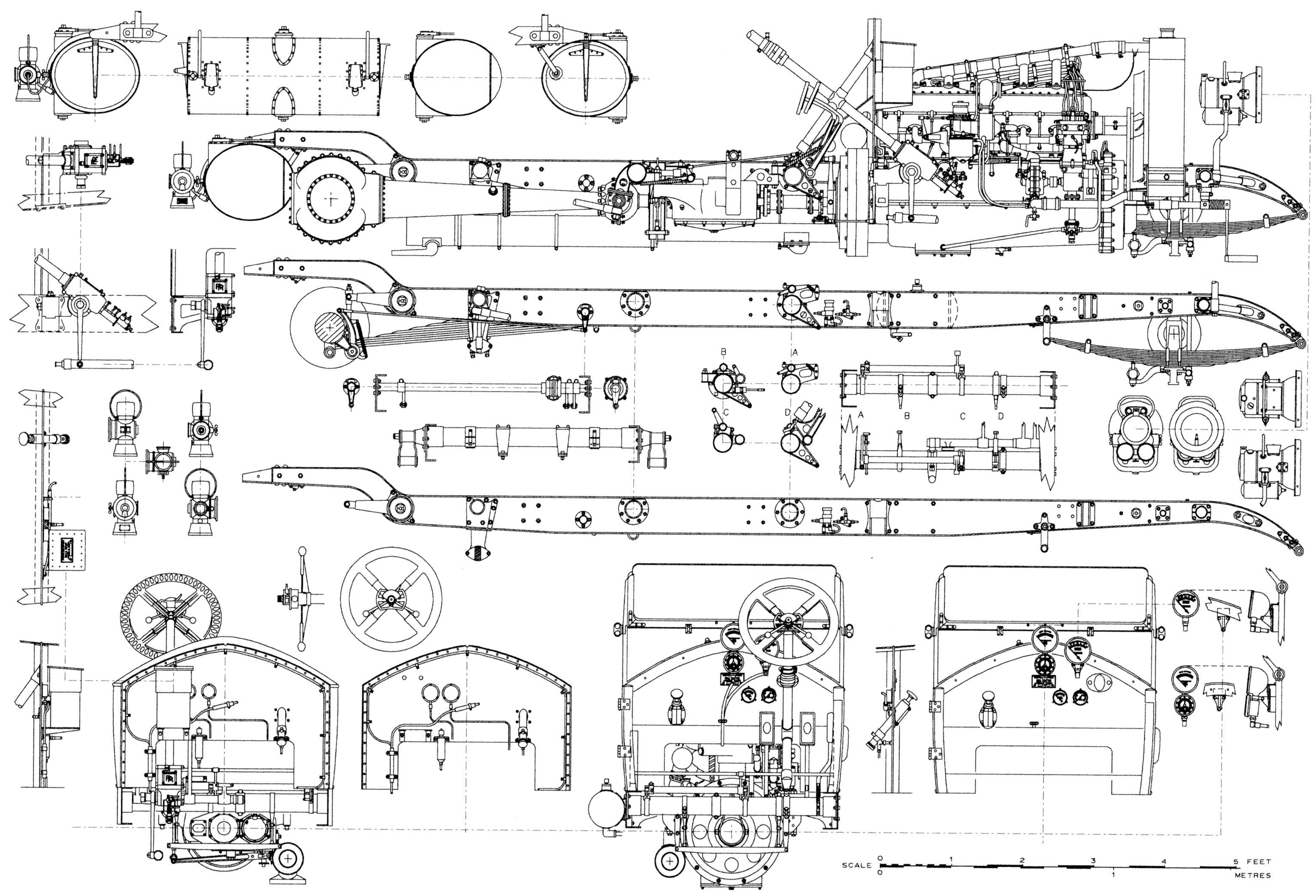

Drafted on Bentley Systems MicroStation©

1912 40/50 Rolls-Royce London-Edinburgh Tourer.

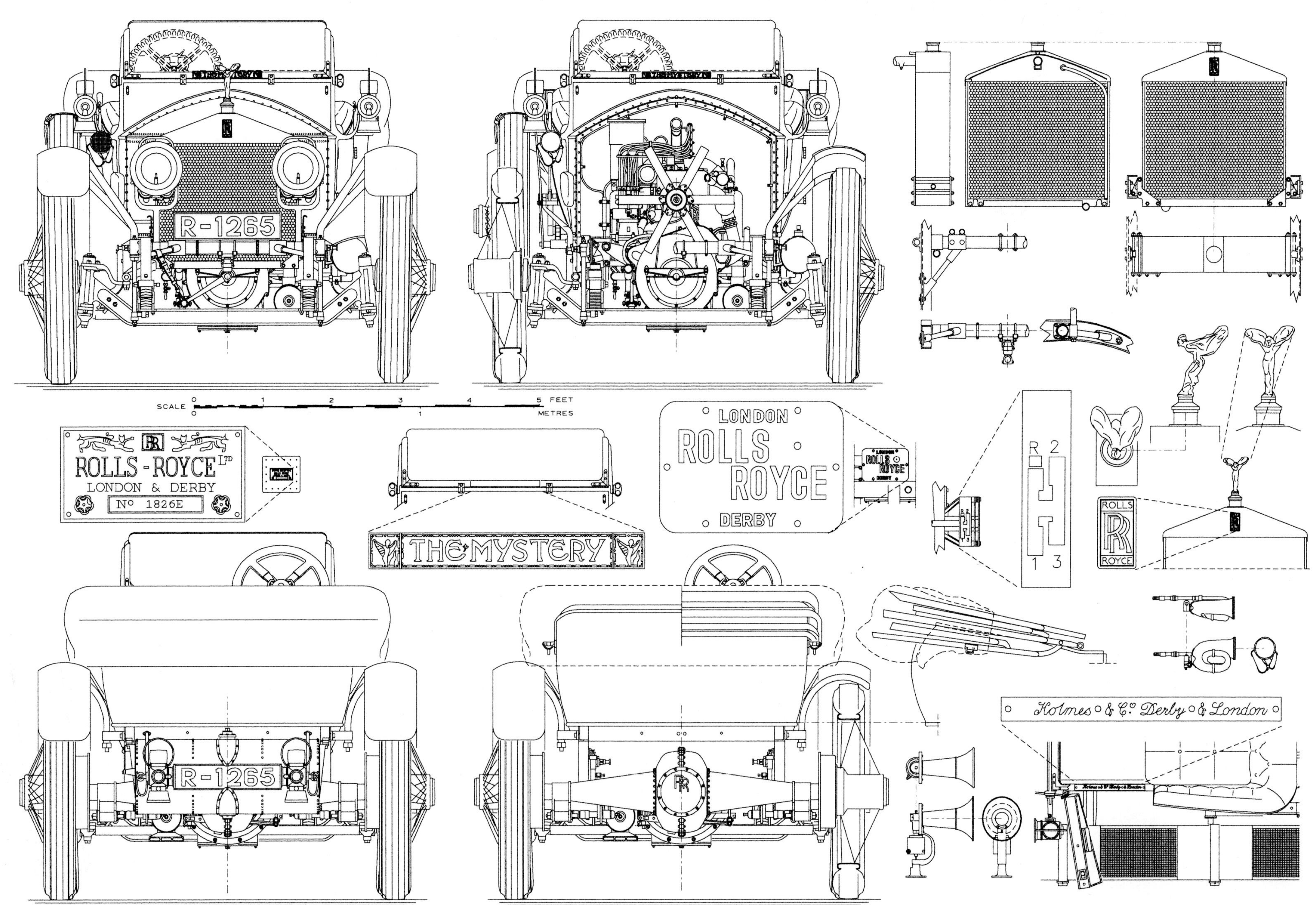

1912 40/50 Rolls-Royce London-Edinburgh Tourer.

Drafted on Bentley Systems MicroStation©

Phyllis & Gerald A Wingrove ©1995

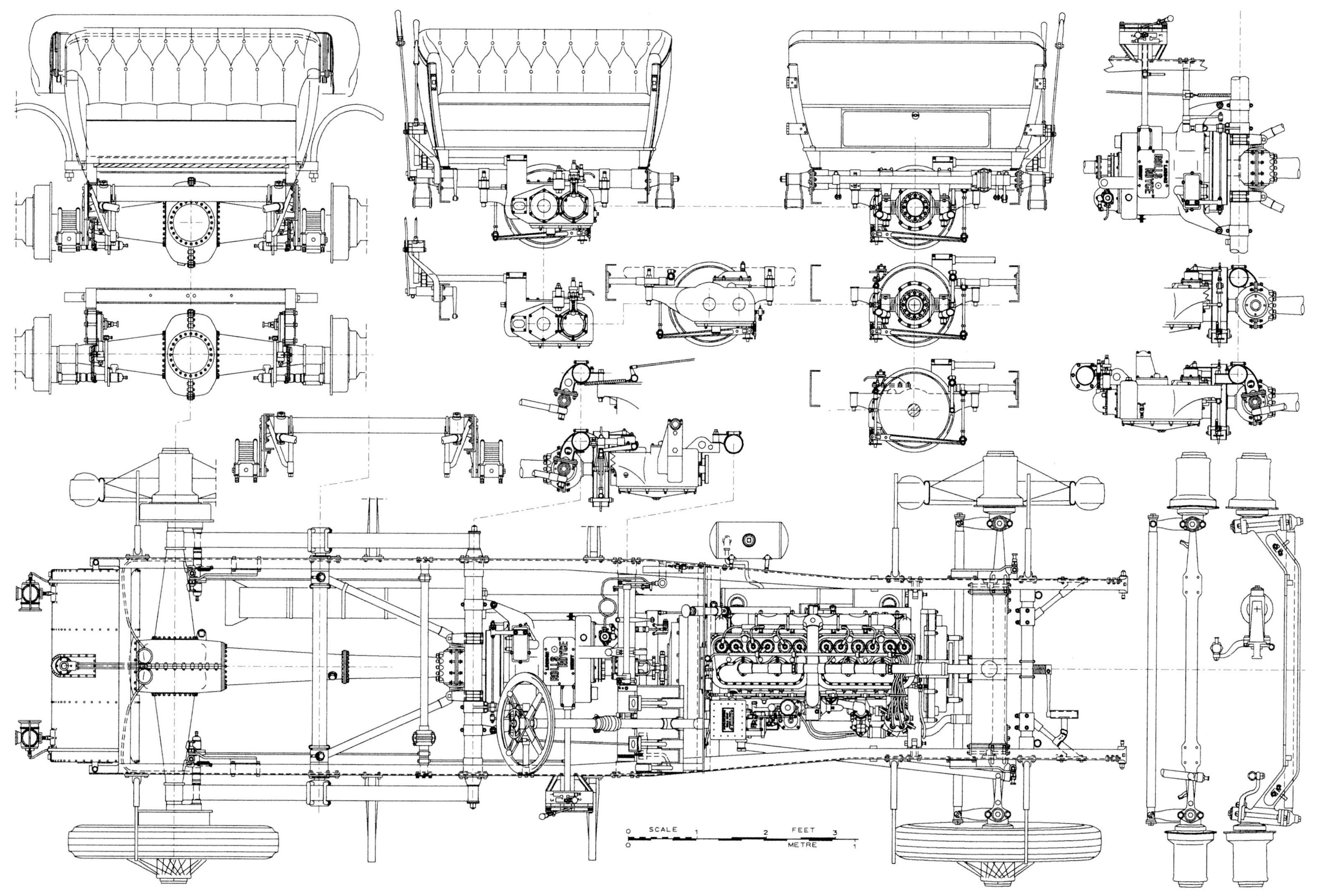

1912 40/50 Rolls-Royce London-Edinburgh Tourer.

Drafted on Bentley Systems MicroStation©

Phyllis & Gerald A Wingrove ©1995

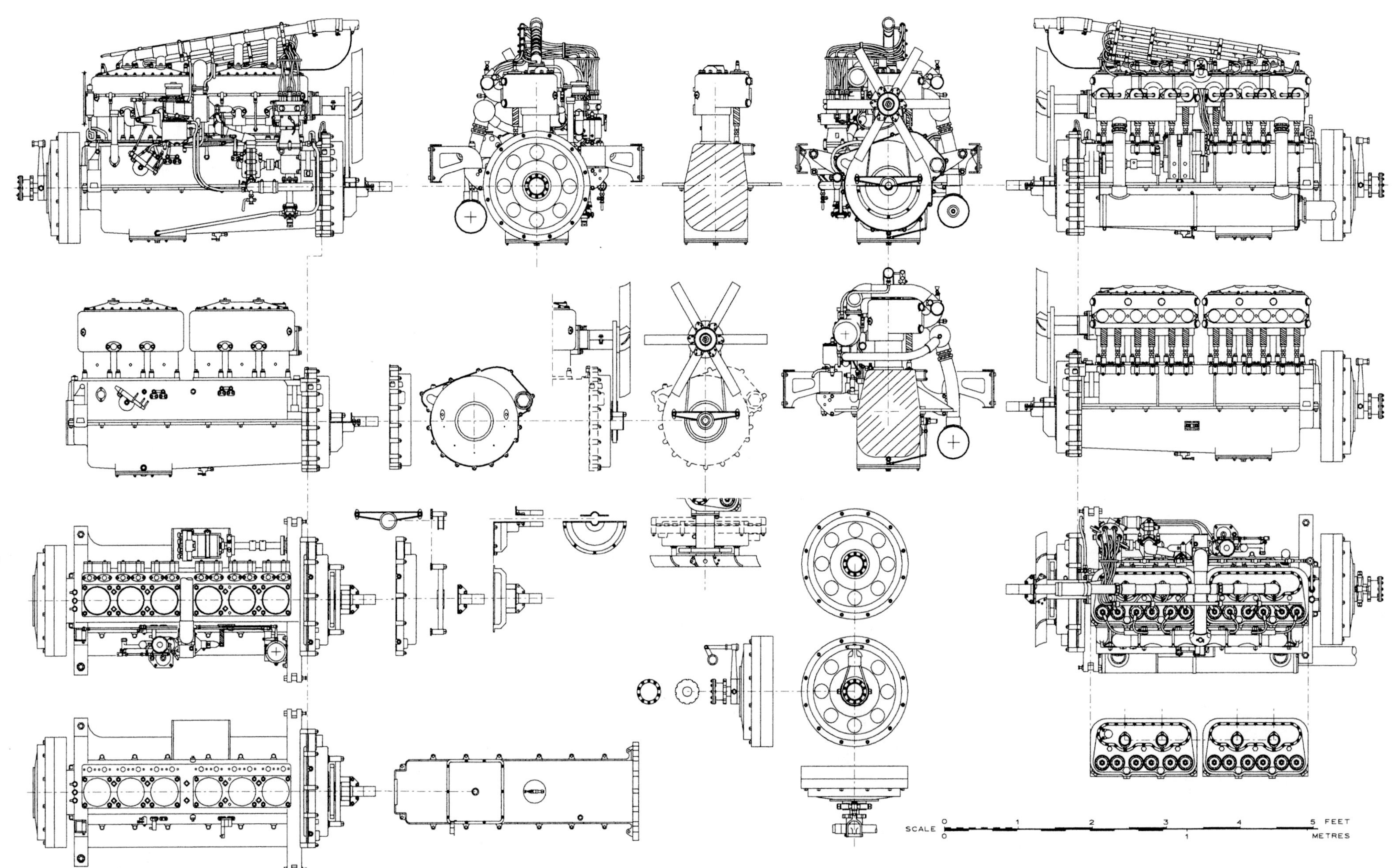

Drafted on Bentley Systems MicroStation©

1912 40/50 Rolls-Royce London-Edinburgh Tourer.

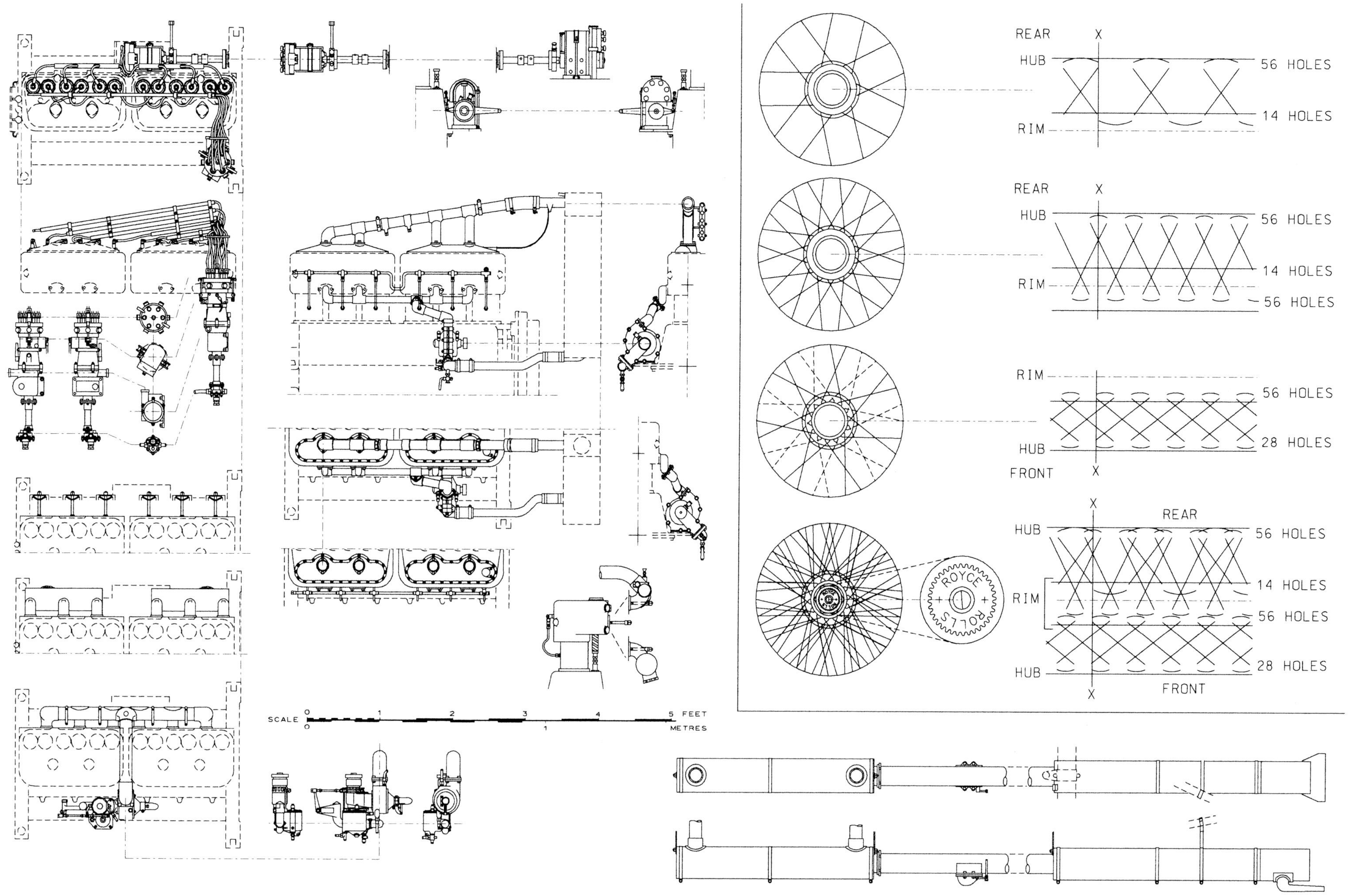

Drafted on Bentley Systems MicroStation©

1912 40/50 Rolls-Royce London-Edinburgh Tourer.

Appendix

Full list of automobile miniatures built in scales of one-twentieth and one-fifteenth of an inch

The date denotes the years when the first model was built. Models built before 1980 are signed Gerald A. Wingrove. Those built between 1980 and 2000 are signed Phyllis & Gerald A. Wingrove. Those built after 2000 are signed with MBE after the signature. 'C' denotes curbside model, 'E' those built with engine and chassis detail.

Order made	Subject	Scale	Date first built	Models made
1	1967 Repco-Brabham BT 24 F1	1:20	C 1968	1
2	1913 Vauxhall Prince Henry two-seater	1:20	C 1968	1
3	1924 Vauxhall 30-98	1:20	C 1968	2
4	1925 'Duck's Back' Alvis 12/50	1:20	C 1968	2
5	1914 Vauxhall Prince Henry 4/5-seater	1:20	C 1968	2
6	1968 Gold Leaf Team Lotus F1	1:20	C 1969	2
7	1912 Mercer Raceabout	1:20	C 1969	10
8	1927 Amilcar CGSS	1:20	C 1969	2
9	1930 Invicta 4.2-Litre S-Type	1:20	C 1969	3
10	1929 Blower Bentley 4.5-litre long chassis	1:20	C 1970	3
11	1930 Bentley 8-litre Special	1:20	C 1970	1
12	1927 Bugatti Type 43	1:20	C 1970	3
13	1930 Brooklands Riley	1:20	C 1970	2
14	1932 Frazer Nash TT Replica	1:20	C 1970	3
15	1969 Matra-Ford F1	1:20	C 1971	2
16	1963 Ferrari 250 GTO	1:15	E 1971	3
17	1964 Ferrari 250 GTO	1:15	C 1971	1
18	1964 Ferrari 250 GTO	1:15	E 1971	2
19	1912 Ford Model 'T' four-seater	1:15	C 1971	1
20	1913 Ford Model 'T' two-seater	1:15	E 1972	3

Order made	Subject	Scale	Date first built	Models Made
21	1927 Stutz Black Hawk Speedster	1:20	C 1972	1
22	1928 Stutz Black Hawk Speedster	1:20	C 1972	2
23	1933 MG J2, cycle wings	1:20	C 1972	1
24	1933 MG J2, swept wings	1:20	C 1972	3
25	1935 Aston Martin Ulster	1:20	C 1972	3
26	1971 Tyrell Ford F1	1:20	C 1973	5
27	1972 JPS Lotus F1	1:20	C 1973	9
28	1924 Hispano-Suiza Nieuport, wood wings	1:15	E 1973	11
29	1924 Hispano-Suiza Nieuport, alum. swept wings	1:15	E 1973	2
30	1924 Hispano-Suiza Nieuport, black swept wings	1:15	E 1973	4
31	1929 Blower Bentley 4.5-litre short chassis	1:15	E 1974	6
32	1930 Alfa Romeo 1750	1:20	C 1974	4
33	1930 Lea-Francis Hyper Sports	1:20	C 1974	2
34	1974 McLaren M23 F1	1:20	C 1975	4
35	1934 Lagonda M45	1:20	C 1975	3
36	1911 Russo-Baltique	1:15	E 1975	4
37	1933 Duesenberg 'J', 'SJ' fully detailed chassis	1:15	E 1976	4
38	1933 Duesenberg 'J' Derham Tourster 2-tone Green	1:15	E 1976	6
39	1931 Duesenberg 'J' Derham Tourster 2-tone Blue	1:15	E 1976	1
40	1975 Ferrari 312 F1	1:20	C 1977	7
41	1932 Alfa Romeo P3 GP	1:15	E 1979	9
42	1933 Duesenberg 'SJ' Weymann Speedster	1:15	C 1979	3
43	1933 Duesenberg 'SJ' Weymann Speedster	1:15	E 1980	6
44	1938 Bugatti Type 57sc Atlantic	1:15	E 1981	9
45	1938 Bugatti Type 57Ssc Atlantic	1:15	C 1982	2
46	1938 Bugatti Type 57sc chassis	1:15	E 1982	1
47	1934 Bugatti Type 59 GP	1:15	E 1982	9

ORDER MADE	SUBJECT	SCALE	DATE FIRST BUILT	MODELS MADE
48	1931 Alfa Romeo 8C 2300 Touring two-seater	1:15	E 1983	7
49	1929 Blower Bentley 4.5-litre long chassis	1:15	E 1984	3
50	1935 Duesenberg 'SSJ'	1:15	E 1988	5
51	1929 Duesenberg 'J' Derham Tourster Yel. & Green	1:15	E 1988	4
52	1931 Duesenberg 'J' chassis	1:15	E 1988	3
53	1938 Bugatti Type 57sc Corsica	1:15	E 1988	5
54	1932 Bugatti Type 41 Weinberger Royale	1:15	E 1988	8
55	1932 Duesenberg 'SJ' Brunn Torpedo Phaeton	1:15	E 1989	2
56	1932 Bugatti Type 41 chassis	1:15	E 1990	2
57	1931 Duesenberg 'J' Derham Tourster B. & Orange	1:15	E 1991	1
58	1933 Duesenberg 'J' Rollston Conv. Coupé	1:15	E 1991	1
59	1933 Duesenberg 'SJ' Walker LaGrande T.Ph.	1:15	E 1993	1
60	1931 Blower Bentley by Gurney Nutting	1:15	E 1994	2
61	1933 Duesenberg 'J' Rollston Conv. Victoria	1:15	E 1994	1
62	1912 Rolls-Royce 40/50 'The Mystery'	1:15	E 1995	3
63	1933 Duesenberg 'J' Murphy Boat Tail Sp.	1:15	E 1995	1
64	1938 Cord 812 Convertible Coupé (rumble seat)	1:15	E 1996	1
65	1938 Cord 812 chassis	1:15	E 1996	1
66	1938 Cord 812 Supercharged Convertible Coupé	1:15	E 1996	1
67	1938 Alfa Romeo 2.9 Touring Cream & Red	1:15	E 1998	1
68	1938 Alfa Romeo 2.9 Mille Miglia	1:15	E 1999	2
69	1938 Alfa Romeo 2.9 chassis	1:15	E 1999	2
70	1938 Alfa Romeo 2.9 Touring Black & Red	1:15	E 1999	1
71	1924 Replica Hispano Suiza in Tulipwood	1:15	E 1999	1
72	1938 Alfa Romeo 2.9 Touring Grey & Red	1:15	E 2000	1

A total of 221 miniature have been hand made between November 1968 and November 2002 by Gerald A. and Phyllis Wingrove Model Engineers (England).

Other books by Gerald A. Wingrove include:

The Complete Car Modeller Volume 1
The Complete Car Modeller Volume 2
The Model Cars of Gerald Wingrove
Unimat Lathe Projects
The Techniques of Ship Modelling

Website: www.geraldwingrove.com.

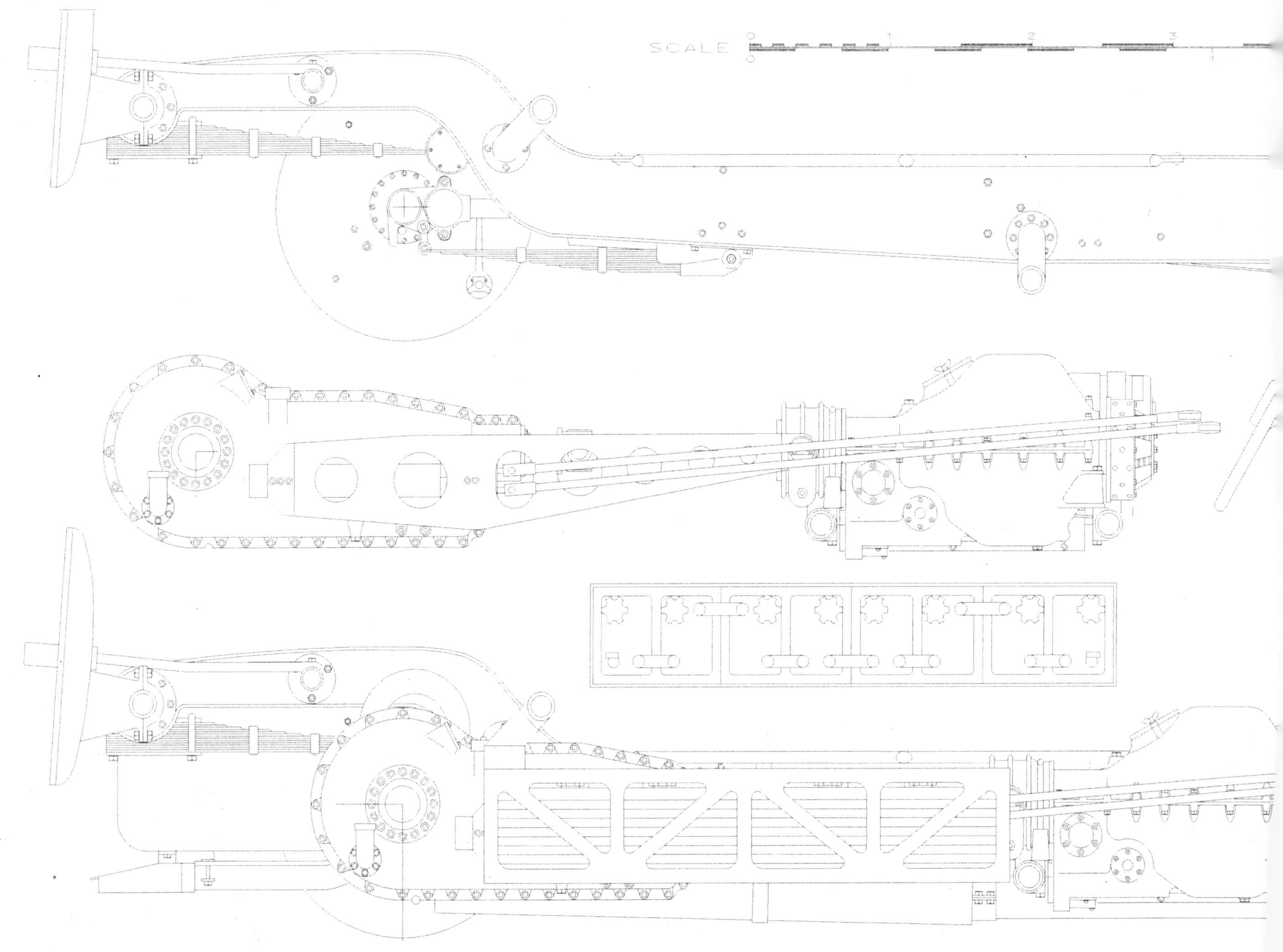
SCALE
0
1
2
3
0
1